# AMERICAYESTERDAY&TODAY

THIS IS A CARLTON BOOK

Text and design copyright © 2002
Carlton Books Limited

This edition published by Carlton
Books Limited 2002
20 Mortimer Street
London
W1T 3JW

ISBN 1 84222 577 4

Editor: Claire Richardson
Art direction: Vicky Holmes
Picture research: Sally Claxton
Production: Janette Burgin

Printed in Singapore

# AMERICA YESTERDAY & TODAY

## BLYTHE HAMER

CARLTON
BOOKS

# CONTENTS

The idea for *America Yesterday & Today* germinated in the aftermath of September 11, 2001, born from the surge of patriotism that all of us felt after the events of that awful morning. Faced with a catastrophic loss of life and a changed world, everyday life in America seemed a blessing that should be savored. The mis-steps of politicians, the teetering stock market, and even a spate of shark attacks—events that took center stage before September 11 —receded in the face of the catastrophe. We re-examined our values, our priorities, and our roots.

Instead of faltering after September 11, we are adjusting, both materially and emotionally. The world today is different, but we are adapting and will continue to do so, just as we did after World War II, the civil rights movement, and the technology revolution. The picture of America that emerges from these pages is a nation with an incredible ability both to effect change and to evolve in the face of change. It is this capability that makes us so resilient.

Change isn't often portrayed as a good thing—an uncomfortable present can make people nostalgic for things they've never even

experienced. You'll find that everything in these pages has altered to some extent over the years, and in all of these changes there is something positive. The development of the Internet, streamlined manufacturing, and vaccines that have eradicated diseases are obvious examples. But did you know that New York City has less air pollution now than it did 50 years ago, or that there are more bears roaming the continent today than there were during colonial times? Richmond, Virginia, once the capital of the Confederacy and a stronghold of slavery, elected the first African–American governor in the country in 1990.

The images portrayed in this book do not claim to present a comprehensive picture of the evolution of America over the past century—it would take thousands of pages to accomplish that lofty goal. However, the breadth, richness and diversity of images contained within these pages provide a valuable insight into the American character and lifestyle and prove that if history, or even recent events, are any indication, we have nothing to fear and much to celebrate.

free time

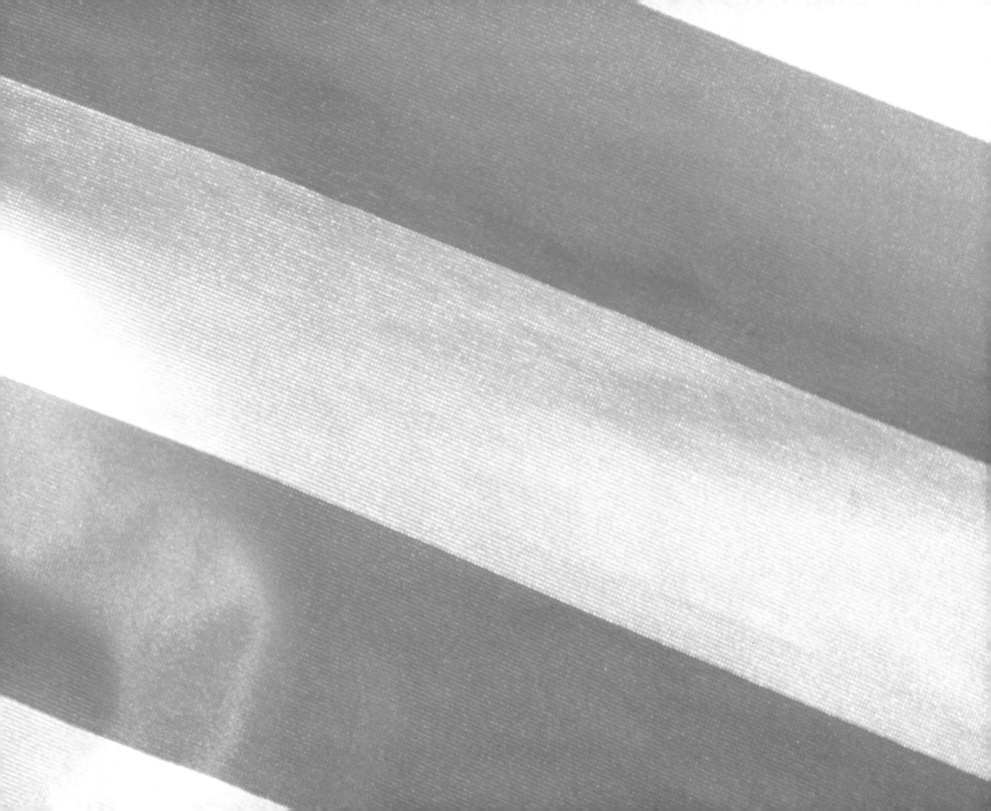

# ROLLER COASTERS

Riders enjoying the thrill of a roller coaster in Palisades Park, New Jersey.

There are few things more fun than screaming your lungs out with a mixture of fear and pleasure—hence the appeal of the roller coaster. The first one, built in Coney Island in 1884, earned $600 a day (at a nickel a ride) and paid for itself in three weeks.

The first ride to flip passengers upside down in a vertical loop was the Flip-Flap in 1895 in Brooklyn, New York—named perhaps because the high G-forces in its circular loop often snapped passengers' necks. In 1901, the Loop-the-Loop in Atlantic City reduced the problem by using an elliptical-shaped pattern, easing neck strain. However, passengers still faced the possibility of falling in the event of an unforeseen stop at the top of the loop. The vertical loops were eventually torn down because they were unsafe.

A new era in roller coasters began when wooden tracks were replaced with steel for the first time in 1959. This technical development made it possible for wheels to hug the track, preventing cars from falling. Coaster designers began making the rides with longer drops and more steeply pitched angles, and loops were successfully reintroduced in 1975. Speeds of up to 100 miles per hour have been recorded—roller coasters are not called "scream machines" for nothing.

Modern roller coasters such as this one in Arlington, Texas, often feature 360° loops.

Young girls taking a Campbell Kid baby doll for a stroll in the park in a miniature baby carriage.

Up to the turn of the 20th century, most American dolls had cloth bodies and ceramic heads, but in 1911, Horsman Dolls, Inc., began making composition dolls with "Can't Break 'Em Heads." One of the most popular types of this new doll was the Campbell Kid. Chubby cheeks and a cherubic smile, along with lots of soup advertisements, made these dolls popular with aspiring young mothers for several decades.

Barbie's introduction to the world in 1959, however, initially met with mixed reviews. Her painted face and womanly shape doubtless challenged some notions of what playing with dolls was meant to be. If she were human, her measurements would translate into a 39-inch chest, 21-inch waist, and 33-inch hips. Nonetheless, Mattel, Inc., now sells two Barbie dolls every second, and 90 percent of all American girls in the last 40 years have owned at least one Barbie.

Choosing a Barbie for Christmas is a serious business—should it be "Glamour on the Go" or "Shopping Spree" Barbie?

A lineup of bathing beauties from Mack Sennett's Keystone movie studio, California.

The original swimsuit was, of course, the body itself, and we seem to have come almost full circle. At the turn of the century, however, when it was not yet acceptable for women to swim, the primary goal of a bathing costume was to camouflage the figure. Women wore voluminous dresses just to go wading. Form followed function in the 1920s when women actually began submerging themselves in the water, and found the costumes unbearable. Despite considerable public outcry, corsets and long skirts were abandoned in favor of lighter, skimpier suits. Matching hats were *de rigueur*.

As time passed, suits became sleeker and more functional, until finally, they became almost nonexistent. The bikini was introduced in 1946 by French designer Louis Reard in Paris, and was immortalized in 1960 when Brian Hyland sang "Itsy Bitsy Teenie Weenie Yellow Polka Dot Bikini." The thong appeared in the 1970s and the world has never been the same since.

A bikini contest in Fort Lauderdale, Florida. The bikini was first introduced in 1946 and has been getting smaller ever since.

## CONVERTIBLES 1913

In the beginning, all cars were convertibles, and driving down the open road with the wind in your hair was not so much a dream as a necessity. The first cars in the 1890s were horse-drawn carriages stripped of their steeds and equipped with gasoline engines. Keeping the engine running was the goal, and a roof was an afterthought.

In 1911, the invention of the electric starter made it easier for women and older men to drive cars. With technical improvements such as heaters, attention shifted to comfort. In 1914, the Dodge brothers introduced the first all-steel car, and drafty canvas tops quickly gave way to closed roofs. By 1928, only 10 percent of cars sold were convertibles.

The glamour of the convertible never faded—Grace Kelly traumatized Cary Grant as she sped through turns on a Riviera cliffside road in *To Catch a Thief*. However, despite the romance, fewer and fewer Americans bought convertibles as the years went by. In 1976 Cadillac announced that the Eldorado would be "the last convertible in America."

Fortunately, Cadillac was wrong. When it comes to sex appeal, a convertible is a sure thing, and for many of the huge population of aging baby boomers, buying a convertible is a last stab at youth. As a result, more convertibles were sold in 2000 in the United States than at any other time in history.

An early automobile—all were convertibles at the time—at an overlook at Laurel Canyon in Hollywood, California.

With their undeniable sex appeal, more convertibles are now bought than ever before.

Harley Davidson bikes dominated racing events from the early days of their production.

For Americans, there really is only one type of motorcycle: the Harley Davidson. Since the first Harley was manufactured in 1903 in a small shed in Milwaukee, Wisconsin, up to the present day, Harley Davidson has been the benchmark for motorcycles, dominating the market in a variety of arenas.

During both World War I and World War II, the United States government commissioned motorcycles for their servicemen from Harley Davidson. The company's bikes have also dominated racing events—a Harley was the first motorcycle ever to win a race averaging over 100 miles per hour. They attract *aficionados* such as Malcolm Forbes and Paul Newman, who love the cruising bikes, replete with custom details.

In fact, it is Harley's appeal across social, ethnic, and financial boundaries that makes it so particularly American. Harley introduced what would become the classic, black leather jacket in 1947, and some of that bad-boy image still lingers. Ironically, many of today's buyers are college-educated married men in their early 40s with plenty of money.

All across America's roads, Harley bikers can be seen riding alone or in packs. Some are gray-haired couples, out for a pleasant drive. Others are members of the Harley Owners Group, affectionately known as HOG, which in the year 2000 had over 500,000 members.

A couple sitting on a Harley Davidson on Main Street in Daytona Beach, Florida.

19

# QUILTING 1930s

The quilting bee, like many aspects of pioneer life in America, fulfilled dual roles by meeting both practical and social needs. Of course, inviting several friends to come help sew a quilt made a large project go quickly, but just as important was the chance to socialize. With farms and homesteads often miles apart, quilting allowed women, who rarely got to see one another, plenty of time to share news and chat.

However, simply being a neighbor did not guarantee you an invitation to the bee. Since only seven or eight people could fit around a typical quilting frame, the hostess would invite only those most skillful with needle and thread. Being good at quilting was actually a social asset, assuring you of friendly company and plenty of gossip.

Antique quilts can fetch thousands of dollars today, and are as often seen in a frame on the wall as they are on top of a bed. The quilting bee remains an important activity, still serving the need for busy fingers and a chance to talk. The close ties forged over such work are strong enough to keep some bees together for over 20 years.

Four Cajun women sewing a quilt in Arnaudsville, Louisiana.

The women of a quilting bee hard at work at the Ozark Arts and Crafts Festival in Branson, Missouri.

## 1920 TAKING THE CURE

People used to travel for miles to enjoy the benefits of mineral water, believing that it could cure illness as well as relieve aches and pains. In 1887 Doc Holliday journeyed to Hot Springs in Glenwood Springs, Colorado, seeking respite from his tuberculosis. Although Holliday died six months after his arrival, people today still flock to Hot Springs seeking the soothing waters, which bubble out of the ground at 122°F and are rich in chloride, sodium, sulfates, boron, and calcium.

For those not able to make the journey to a hot spring resort, hot tubs and bottled mineral water abound. In fact, bottled water is about to bypass beer, coffee, and tea to become the second largest-selling beverage in the country, after soft drinks. Americans guzzle more than 18 gallons of bottled water per person every year, even though a recent study by the World Wildlife Fund International states that bottled water is no healthier than what comes out of the faucet—and it costs up to 1,000 times more.

Drinking mineral water at Hot Springs in Glenwood Springs, Colarado was believed to provide relief from all manner of ailments, ranging from tuberculosis to fatigue.

A woman enjoys a hot tub and a cold bottle of water at a spa resort in Tuscon, Arizona.

America experienced a broadcasting boom in the 1920s, and family and friends would gather around the radio to listen to favorite programs.

Radio was invented at the turn of the 20th century, but it was not until the development of the vacuum-tube radio transmitter in 1915 that widespread broadcasting became possible. By 1917, when the United States entered World War I, radio was considered so important to the dissemination of information that the government closed or took over all private radio stations. It was illegal for a citizen even to possess a radio transmitter, for fear that it would be misused by spies.

After 1919, when the restrictions on civilian radio were lifted, a broadcasting boom swept the country. The number of stations nationwide grew in 1922 from 67 to over 500, and programming included amateur talent, readings from books, live music performances, and commentary. For many people, particularly rural dwellers, a radio provided the only link to the outside world. Entire families sat down in the living room to listen to favorite broadcasts.

While listening to the radio is no longer a formal event, it is still a popular one, despite the introduction of competing media such as television and the Internet. Small radios attach to armbands or belts, so that we can tune in while jogging, commuting, or even going to the supermarket.

The advent of smaller technology means that listening to the radio is no longer a sedentary pastime.

The arrival of a bookmobile such as this one in Randolph County, North Carolina, was an eagerly anticipated event, bringing a world of information and entertainment to small towns and rural areas.

Bookmobiles came into widespread use in the 1940s and 1950s to serve people living in rural areas far away from public libraries. Often makeshift, bookmobiles took a variety of forms. Many had panels on the outside that could be opened so that people could choose from the books inside. They parked at gas stations, public schools, private homes, drugstores, and prisons, bringing books to isolated people hungry for a glimpse of the world beyond their town.

In the 1960s, the need in rural areas diminished as television became more widespread and people began moving in greater numbers to urban areas. Bookmobiles became common in cities, where they served disadvantaged people such as those in housing developments and nursing homes.

Today, the Internet has profoundly changed the way people receive information. With a telephone or cable television line, anyone can dial up the world in a second. Even visitors to the library will often use computers instead of books. Bookmobiles still exist, however, and they are a lifesaver for those without access to computers and far away from any library. Some bookmobiles are even equipped with computers and Internet access.

Reading on screen rather than paper is now commonplace. The combination of coffee and computers in Internet cafés such as this one in Times Square, New York City, is very popular.

This picture is from *Television: Promise and Problem*, an early pamphlet about the positive and negative influences of television.

During the 1950s, television became the dominant form of mass media in America. Much the way families had gathered around the radio in the 1920s, they now sat together in the living room to watch television. The development in 1951 of coaxial cable and coast-to-coast microwave relays meant that stations could broadcast live news events. People began to accept what they heard on television as fact because they were often eyewitnesses. In 1954, color television was introduced.

Youngsters watched television more hours than they went to school, a trend that has not changed much over time. Popular shows such as *Father Knows Best* and *The Adventures of Ozzie and Harriet* portrayed ideal families and schools. *The Ed Sullivan Show*, broadcast on Sunday evenings, brought The Beatles into American homes.

Today, 99 percent of American households have televisions. Cable TV has given rise to hundreds of specialty networks on sports, cooking, history, and even shopping. So-called "reality" game shows like *Survivor* have replaced idealized versions of life, and popular programs sometimes tackle tough questions on topics such as homosexuality, violence, and racism.

The popularity of television never wanes—virtually every household in America has at least one TV.

George Eastman (left) and Thomas Edison, whose inventions (celluloid film and a projector, respectively) played a crucial role in the birth of the movies.

George Eastman and Thomas Edison each contributed inventions critical to the creation of a new art form—the motion picture. Aware that paper film broke too easily inside cameras, in 1889 Eastman began manufacturing flexible, transparent film on a celluloid base. The 35-mm wide, perforated rolls of film allowed an assistant in Edison's laboratories to develop the Kinetograph in 1893, which used an incandescent bulb (another of Edison's inventions) to illuminate photographs that flickered past an eyehole. The first "motion picture" was made—a re-creation of a sneeze.

Early movies were between 30 and 60 seconds long, and showed nameless actors in everyday scenes from life—a kiss, the activities of a fire fighter, or workers leaving a factory. However, films soon evolved into longer narrative stories, including fictional plots, character development, and trick photography. Nameless actors became movie stars, and by the 1920s the American public was flocking to movie palaces to see favorites such as Mary Pickford.

People are still fascinated by movie stars and eagerly consume the pictures and gossip about them that abounds in today's media. Photographers swarm celebrities, trying to capture revealing moments on film, and have become known as *paparazzi*, after a character in Federico Fellini's 1960 movie *La Dolce Vita*.

Photographers trying to get the perfect shot at the O.J. Simpson trial in Santa Monica, California.

# FITNESS

Elderly ladies listening to music on a gramophone at the Jones-Harrison rest home in Minneapolis.

Most of us today expect to enjoy an active old age. In the early years of the 20th century, however, sedate activities such as listening to music were the most an elderly person might be expected to do, with an occasional stroll around the porch for the more sprightly.

Nowadays, most of us are all too aware of the health benefits of exercise. Aging baby boomers, in particular, are devoting more free time than ever to staying fit. Unfortunately, they have also experienced significantly more sports-related injuries—a 33 percent increase from 1991 to 1998. These adults are playing sports more seriously at older ages, and most of the injuries that occur are caused by years of athletic wear and tear combined with aging tissues that are more susceptible to injury. Experts are dubbing the new phenomenon "boomeritis," so-called because the most common complaints are "itis" ailments like bursitis, tendinitis, and arthritis.

The best way to ward off these problems is to improve flexibility by working on exercises that both strengthen and stretch muscles. Another strategy is to add some rest days into the overall fitness routine. After all, our ancestors were probably not all wrong.

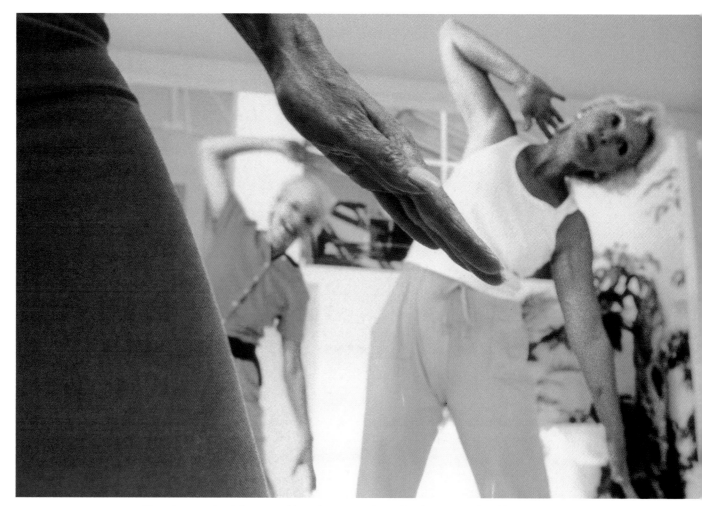

Nowadays, people of all ages participate in sports and exercise classes—growing older is no longer a barrier.

# PLAYING GAMES

Young fans of the *Davy Crockett* TV show act out their hero's adventures in the wild frontier of the back yard.

It is hard to remember the days when a single person could capture and hold the imagination of a generation of children. However, that is what happened in 1954 when the new Walt Disney show *Davy Crockett Indian Fighter* aired on ABC-TV.

David Crockett was a real man, a legend in his own time in the early 1800s, who was a famous hunter and politician. He died a hero's death fighting at the Alamo. No one, however, anticipated how popular the television show would become. That famous song helped— "Davy, Davy Crockett, king of the wild frontier!"—and the demand for coonskin caps was so great that the price of the fur more than tripled.

Today, having a toy gun at school can be cause for arrest, and the wild frontier is a concept most children do not understand. Hunting more likely takes the form of searching for aliens on video games. Nintendo, one of the leaders in the video game industry, claims that more than 40 percent of American households own a Nintendo game system.

The enthrallment of virtual reality—from dinosaurs to aliens, there's a video game to spark every child's imagination.

This photograph of a young child gazing in wonder at Sleeping Beauty Castle was taken a few days before the grand opening of Disneyland, California.

# DISNEYLAND 1955

When Disneyland opened in Anaheim, California, in 1955, it was unique not just because of its size and scope, the likes of which had never been seen before. It broke new ground because it contained none of the traditional attractions found in amusement parks, such as Ferris wheels.

Fantasyland, with its Sleeping Beauty Castle, was just one of five theme areas where visitors could travel. Frontierland, another popular spot, was designed so that guests could relive the pioneer days of the American frontier. Tomorrowland was created as a look at the "marvels of the future," though Walt Disney worried right from the start that it would be instantly outdated.

Disneyland was a hit when it opened, despite a disastrous heat wave that made the newly laid, still-damp asphalt cling to high-heeled shoes. Other theme parks sprang up around the country, and spurred renewed interest in amusement parks as well. Today, there are Disneylands in Paris and Tokyo, and a Disney World in Florida. Millions have experienced Walt Disney's vision, and a trip to one is becoming a rite of passage for American children.

Sleeping Beauty Castle forms the entrance to Fantasyland, one of the five theme areas of Disneyland. It is as popular with adult visitors as it is with children.

# 1950

## PLAYING TO WIN

A woman playing a 5-cent slot machine in Reno, Nevada. One-armed bandits were first introduced in casinos to entertain wives and girlfriends.

Although an American named Charles Fey invented the slot machine in 1894, the machines did not reach Las Vegas until the 1940s, when Bugsy Siegel added them to his Flamingo hotel.

People love playing slot machines because, unlike other casino games, they do not require any skill. Known affectionately as one-armed bandits because of the lever at the side of the machine that is used to set the reels spinning, the goal is to get the symbols on all reels lined up on the payline in a winning combination. The more reels and the more symbols, the harder it is to win. Although the early mechanical machines with three old-style reels holding 20 symbols are still around, many casinos have replaced them with microprocessor-controlled video screens simulating multiple reels and hundreds of symbols.

Slot machines were originally installed to entertain the wives and girlfriends of high rollers, but they were so popular that casinos began making more money off them than from their regular table games. Now, slot machines account for over two-thirds of casino revenue in the United States.

The hundreds of slot machines in this Las Vegas casino reflect the fact that they generate over two-thirds of all casino revenue.

# KITCHENS

Early advertisers promised to free the 1950s housewife from banal domestic chores with their new electric stoves, refrigerators, and dishwashers.

Early advertisers promised to free the 1950s housewife from banal domestic chores with their new electric stoves, refrigerators, and dishwashers.

Body piercing has been around for millennia—a 5,000-year-old mummified body found in a glacier had pierced ears. Piercing spans all races and cultures, from jungle tribes of South America to European aristocrats of the 19th century. Sailors used to have an ear pierced because it was supposed to improve eyesight, but an added benefit was that a gold earring on a corpse could pay for a burial. Julius Caesar and William Shakespeare wore gold rings in their ears. In Borneo, ear piercing is a puberty ritual, where the mother and father of a child each pierce one ear as a symbol of the child's dependence on his parents.

In the period after World War II, ear piercing in the United States was considered *risqué*, and women often resorted to their own devices. Necessary tools were a needle to puncture the ear, an ice cube to numb the pain, and a shot of vodka used alternately for needle sterilization and courage. More recently, the fad has been to pierce just about anything, including tongues, navels, eyebrows, and noses. While today's techniques are more refined than they were 50 years ago, the question of how a person with a pierced nose handles a cold remains unanswered.

*Opposite:* This man piercing a client's nose in San Francisco obviously believes in advertising his profession—and that of the tattoo artist next door.

Friends offer moral support to a young woman having her ears pierced in Memphis, Tennessee.

Kitchens are the heart of the home, and their evolution is a barometer of changing domestic life. In the 1940s and 1950s, modern conveniences were being sold as tools to liberate the wife from the banalities of housework. Advertisements depicted kitchen appliances as objects of desire that could be purchased in a variety of colors, including turquoise and pink. The electric dishwasher made its debut, and TV dinners were introduced. The modern mother still served her family meals at the kitchen table, but she used pressurized Reddi Wip as a time-saver.

The color schemes changed—avocado green and harvest gold in the 1960s gave way to neutrals in the 1980s—and new appliances such as the microwave and the food processor were invented. However, women did not shake their roles as doyennes of domesticity until the 1980s when they went to work in large numbers. Kitchen space opened up so that working parents could spend more time with their children, and breakfast bars were created for meals on the go. Today, packaged foods mean that even children can make themselves a hot snack.

In modern homes, cooking and other kitchen chores are no longer the sole responsibility of the woman of the household.

# MUD BATHS

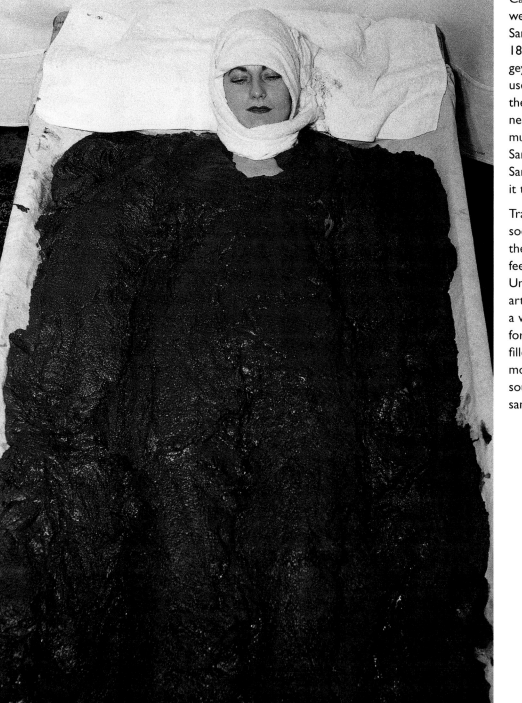

California legend has it that mud baths were the idea of Samuel Brannan, a wealthy San Francisco executive. He realized in 1859 that the hot spring waters and natural geysers in northern Napa Valley could be used to create a perfect resort. He mixed the thermal waters with volcanic ash from nearby Mount St Helena to concoct the first mud baths. Originally, he called the place the Saratoga of California after New York's famous Saratoga Hot Springs, but later he shortened it to Calistoga.

Travelers still escape to Calistoga for its soothing mud baths, made with water from the same geothermal underground lake that feeds the Old Faithful geyser of California. Until recently, mud baths were promoted as an arthritis treatment, but now they are touted as a way to relax. The procedure involves lying for 10 to 15 minutes in a sarcophagus-like tub filled with mud made from volcanic ash, peat moss, clay, and hot spring water. Although it sounds dirty, spa operators claim the mud is sanitary due to the high heat of the water.

With her head swathed in bandages, there is a distinct medicinal air to this woman's mud bath at Arrowhead Springs, California.

The mud baths at Calistoga in California use geothermal underground waters mixed with volcanic ash, peat moss, and clay. Nowadays, they are used for relaxation as much as for their traditional medical benefits.

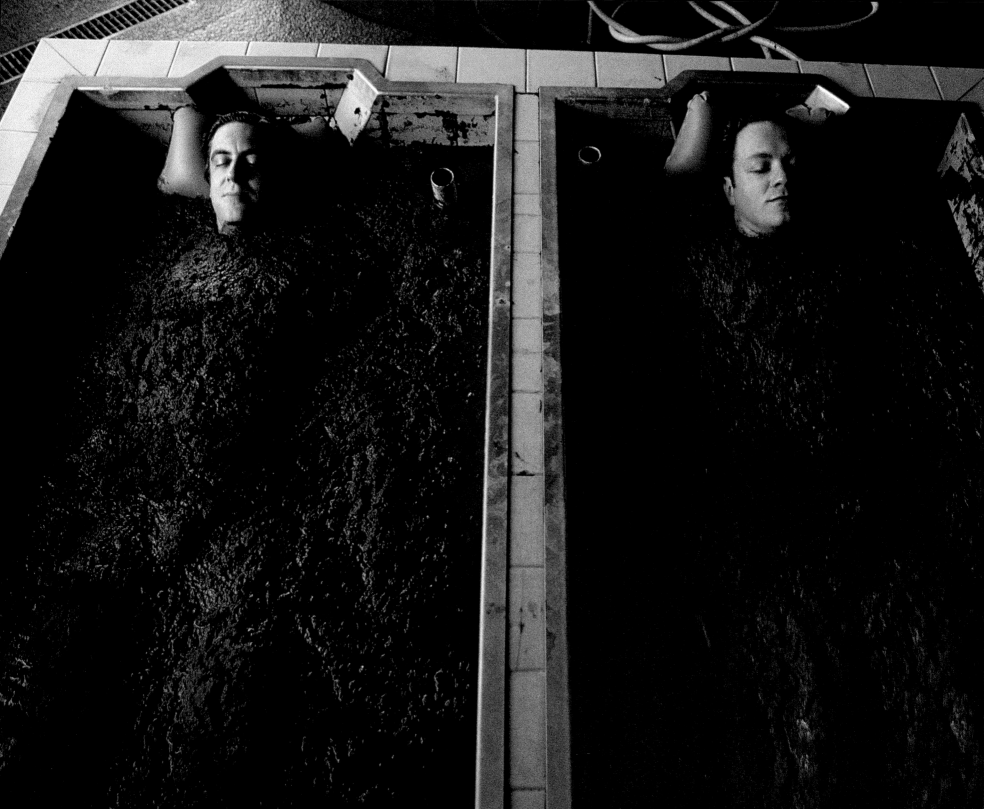

A couple doing the jitterbug at a Salvation Army Christmas benefit—parents hated the sexual energy of such dances.

Swing dancing dates back to the 1920s, when the black community discovered the Charleston and the Lindy Hop while dancing to contemporary Jazz music. In 1934, band leader Cab Calloway introduced a bouncy six beat variant called "Jitterbug".

Jitterbug contests were extremely popular with American teenagers. For example on June 18, 1939, over 1,000 contestants entered "The International Swing Jam"—the largest ever sponsored jitterbug contest, which took place at the Los Angeles Coliseum.

By the 1980s teenagers had developed a new form of self-expressions—the mosh pit. A swirling circle of gyrating youths, the mosh pit forms in front of the stage at concerts. The mosh pit cannot really be called dancing, since the chaos of churning arms and legs has no discernible rhyme or reason, and injuries and even deaths have been attributed to the practice. Offshoots of the mosh pit include stage diving, when a person dives off the stage into the audience, and crowd surfing, when the audience picks somebody up and passes them along until they are set down some distance away.

New dances and music-related crazes continue to emerge, such as crowd surfing, where audience members at concerts pass someone along overhead.

## FASHION 1968

A fashion revolution occurred in the 1960s. Tired of their parents' clothes, and bored by seeing pop singers in gowns and actresses in gloves, people were ready for something dramatically different.

A new breed of fashion designer was inspired by the space age and Pop art to introduce big geometric patterns, fur vests and coats, bell-bottoms, and "go-go" boots. However, it was the miniskirt that was the decade's defining fashion statement. Mary Quant, the British designer credited with inventing the style, attributed its popularity to "the girls on the street," saying that working women, not fashion designers, were ultimately the trendsetters.

It is still the kids on the street who set the styles. While the miniskirt makes regular comebacks, new fashions have emerged. Skateboarders hanging out in parking lots and school playgrounds have popularized a hip-hop style characterized by baggy pants pooled at the ankles, oversized T-shirts, and Airwalk sneakers.

Movie and music stars help to create and popularize new fashion trends. This picture of Sonny and Cher walking around New York City is the epitome of 1960s chic.

Skateboard style, characterized by baggy pants and sneakers, exemplifies the contemporary preference for casual clothes.

# american classics

Steelworkers from Warren, Ohio, demonstrate against a foreign takeover bid outside the Capitol in Washington, D.C., with the help of Uncle Sam.

Uncle Sam was born plain old Samuel Wilson in 1766 in Arlington, Massachusetts. He served as a drummer boy and a soldier during the Revolutionary War, and in 1789 he moved to Troy, New York, where he built a thriving slaughterhouse and meat packing business. He was fair and honest, and became known affectionately as "Uncle Sam."

During the War of 1812, he provided barrels of beef and pork to the army troops camped outside his town. To designate that they were for the army and not for general sale, he stamped each barrel with "U.S." The terms U.S. and U.S.A. were not yet in general use, though, so a member of a federal inspection crew visiting Wilson's plant one day asked a workman what the letters stood for. "Probably Uncle Sam," said the worker.

It did not take long for people to begin using the nickname Uncle Sam to mean the federal government. Although Sam Wilson was tall and thin, the first drawings showed a portly Uncle Sam, dressed in black top hat and tails. Later, his clothing was drawn in the colors of the flag. Finally, he became tall and bearded, after cartoonists began modeling him on Abraham Lincoln. His most famous role was in a recruiting poster for World War I, where he utters the famous "I Want You." Today, he remains a sometimes serious, sometimes humorous symbol of the United States.

Uncle Sam in the Buffalo Bill Cody
Stampede Parade in Cody, Wyoming.

A demonstrator offers a flower to military police on guard at the Pentagon during an anti-Vietnam demonstration in Arlington, Virginia.

Protests have long been a mainstay of American politics, but the biggest anti-war demonstrations in American history occurred in the 1960s when people came from all over the country to Washington, D.C., to rally against the Vietnam War. The first Washington rally in 1965 was largely peaceful, and only four arrests were made. By October1967, however, 13,000 Americans had died in Vietnam, and over 100,000 protestors converged to march on the Pentagon, inflamed with moral certainty that the war was wrong.

Norman Mailer and Abbie Hoffman were among the 681 people arrested in the march—most for disorderly conduct and breaking police lines. Soldiers brandishing M-14 rifles were approached by hippies, who offered flowers as a symbol of their plea for peace. U.S. combat troops pulled out of Vietnam in 1972, in part because of the strength of America's anti-war sentiment.

Now, tree huggers have replaced flower children. They were among the many activists protesting against the World Trade Organization in Seattle in November 1999. There, 20,000 demonstrators succeeded in stopping the organization's opening conference day and in drawing national attention to their concern that growing global trade is harming the environment and increasing human rights violations.

A protestor prays in front of a line of police in a demonstration against international financial policy and globalization.

Academy Award winner Shirley Temple presents Walt Disney with an Oscar and seven miniature statuettes for *Snow White and the Seven Dwarfs*.

The Academy Awards, known affectionately as the Oscars after the statues presented to winners, were first awarded in 1927. Although the ceremonies are held to honor the best films, their real attraction lies in offering a glimpse of the stars.

At the 1938 Academy Awards (presented in February 1939), two of the brightest stars were Shirley Temple and Walt Disney. Temple was the box-office champion for three straight years from 1936 to 1938, beating the likes of Clark Gable, Gary Cooper, and Joan Crawford. She presented Walt Disney with an honorary award for *Snow White and the Seven Dwarfs*. The film was the first successful, full-length animated feature, and Disney received one regular Oscar and seven miniature ones. Temple had herself received a miniature Oscar for her contribution to screen entertainment in 1934—she was five years old at the time, and was earning $75 a week.

Julia Roberts and Russell Crowe were the winners of the best actress and actor awards for 2000—both are giant box-office attractions. For her winning role in *Erin Brockovich*, Roberts received $20 million, the highest fee paid to an actress up to that date. Denzel Washington and Halle Berry won the 2001 best actor and actress Oscars at the 74th Academy Awards. They were only the second and third African-Americans to win best acting honors, the first being Sidney Poitier in 1963. Poitier also received an honorary award for his contribution to the motion-picture industry at the 74th Awards.

Best actress winner Julia Roberts and best actor Russell Crowe holding their Oscars at the 73rd Academy Awards.

# THE LINCOLN MEMORIAL 1920

Work on the Lincoln Memorial began in 1915, 50 years after the assassination of President Abraham Lincoln. Lincoln's stewardship of the nation during the Civil War led to the abolishment of slavery, and the memorial is a tribute to one of the greatest American presidents.

The statue was completed in 1922. Sculptor Daniel Chester French had doubled the size of the original piece, realizing that the huge chamber inside the memorial required a larger work than initially planned. He used 28 slabs of white Georgia marble, which were put together for the first time almost seamlessly inside the memorial.

Since then, the memorial has been the backdrop for many public protests. The acclaimed contralto Marian Anderson gave her Easter Sunday concert there in 1939, after being turned away from Constitution Hall by the Daughters of the American Revolution because she was an African–American. Dr Martin Luther King Jr, stood there in 1963 to deliver his "I Have a Dream" speech, and anti-war activists used the steps for rallies protesting against the Vietnam War.

The statue of Abraham Lincoln was constructed on-site from 28 pieces of pre-carved marble. As well as being a popular tourist attraction, the memorial to the anti-slavery president has also provided an appropriate backdrop for many public protests.

The Statue of Liberty was a gift from France to America to commemorate the American and French Revolutions.

# THE STATUE OF LIBERTY

The Statue of Liberty was the dream of a French sculptor named Frédéric-Auguste Bartholdi, who wanted to make a gift of a lasting monument to liberty from the French people to the United States. Inspired by the majestic pyramids during a trip to Egypt, Bartholdi pitched his idea of a colossal statue in New York City's harbor to both Frenchmen and Americans alike.

Although fundraising for the statue began in 1875, money was slow to come in. Joseph Pulitzer, publisher of the *World* newspaper, had a brilliant idea—to print the name of every single contributor in the paper, no matter how small the donation. Money poured in, and Lady Liberty was finally completed in 1884. She arrived in New York on June 15, 1885—packed inside 214 wooden crates.

It took another year to build the foundation for her, but she was finally unveiled on October 28, 1886. The ticker tape parade was born that day, as office boys on Wall Street leaned out of their windows to unreel spools of tape while the celebratory parade marched in the streets below. One hundred years later on July 4, 1986, America held a birthday party for the Statue of Liberty. With millions watching, the statue was illuminated by spotlights and a spectacular fireworks display.

In 1986 a magnificent fireworks display was staged to celebrate the Statue of Liberty's 100th birthday.

## IMMIGRANTS 1930

Early immigrants arrived in New York Harbor to the welcome sight of the Statue of Liberty.

Over 100 million Americans can trace their ancestry to a man, woman, or child who immigrated to the United States from another country.

Early immigrants, arriving in New York Harbor after harrowing transatlantic passages, were greeted with the mythic vision of America—the Statue of Liberty. Then it was on to Ellis Island, where from 1897 to 1938, thousands of immigrants each day were examined by doctors and registered in record books. During the peak years of immigration prior to 1924, around 34 million immigrants landed on American soil.

Although the rate of immigration has slowed, the United States is still seen as a safe haven for many people seeking to escape problems in their native land. Since 1995, for example, the U.S. Immigration and Naturalization Service has granted citizenship to over 130,000 Cubans fleeing from the economic and authoritarian policies of Fidel Castro's government. The 1966 Cuban Adjustment Act allows any Cuban landing on American soil the right to stay while applying for residency—the only group of immigrants allowed this special status.

The United States is a country founded on immigration. Here, Cuban immigrants at a ceremony in Florida raise their right hands and are sworn in as United States citizens.

After personally delivering a letter to the White House offering help in the war on drugs, Elvis Presley was invited to the Oval office to meet President Nixon in person.

# FAMOUS MEETINGS

Two of America's icons, Richard Nixon and Elvis Presley, met in 1970. The meeting was Presley's idea, born of a desire to become the country's first "Federal Agent at Large" to help in the war on drugs. In a six-page letter he handwrote on an American Airlines flight en route from Memphis to Washington, D.C., Presley stated: "The drug culture, the hippie elements, the SDS, Black Panthers, etc. do not consider me as their enemy… I will help out by doing it my way through my communications with people of all ages."

He personally delivered the note to the White House gate. On December 21, Nixon greeted Presley, who was wearing a purple velvet suit with matching cape and a huge gold belt buckle. During the meeting, Presley told Nixon he was "on your side," and later gave him a hug. Presley received a special badge from the Bureau of Narcotics and Dangerous Drugs, although he was never made an agent.

Ricky Martin had no political agenda when he performed at George W. Bush's inauguration ceremony on January 18, 2001. The big moment of the party came when Martin pulled the president-elect on to the stage and tried to get him to dance. Fireworks exploded overhead a few minutes later.

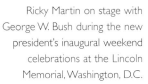

Ricky Martin on stage with George W. Bush during the new president's inaugural weekend celebrations at the Lincoln Memorial, Washington, D.C.

A group of suffragists taking part in the New York Fair's parade proclaim their cause—it took more than 70 years for women to secure the right to vote.

The women's suffrage movement in America lasted more than 70 years, from the first formal women's convention in Seneca Falls, New York, in 1848 to the passage of the 19th amendment in 1920 giving women the right to vote. The movement gained real momentum after the Civil War, when the vote was given to black men. Women became even more determined to win the same right.

It was not until the 1900s, however, that the movement expanded beyond radicals and reached out to socially prominent, middle- and upper-class women with the argument that suffrage would help their civic improvement efforts. Open air meetings, parades, marches, and other forms of active protest drew attention to their efforts.

The League of Women Voters was founded in 1920 just a few months before the 19th amendment was ratified. Its mission was to help 20 million women carry out their new responsibilities as voters. Today, it is a non-partisan, grassroots organization devoted to education and activism. Among its priorities is election administration reform, prompted by the 2000 presidential election, which hinged on the Florida recount. The League is working with members of Congress to develop federal legislation addressing the issues of antiquated voting machines, confusing ballot systems, and a lack of standardization and consistency.

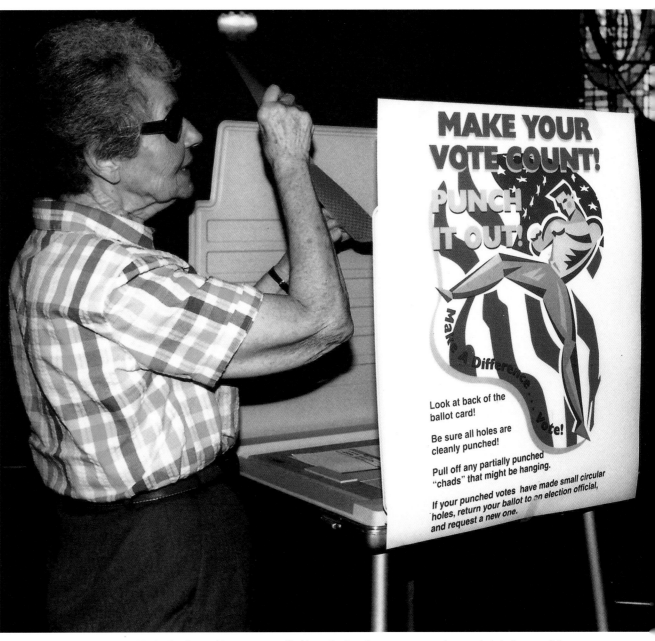

A year after the 2000 presidential election fiasco, this poster on a Florida voting booth urges voters to inspect their ballots carefully.

## MISS AMERICA 1927

Women have long been measured by their looks, but, ironically, the first bathing beauty contest in the United States was not held until 1921, one year after women had finally cast their first votes.

That year, as the summer season in Atlantic City, New Jersey, drew to a close, business leaders came up with an idea to keep visitors in town past Labor Day. They staged a fall festival that included a contest on the beach to select "the most beautiful bathing beauty in America." Eight women paraded down the boardwalk, wearing knee-length bathing suits.

Even then, the pageant had its detractors, with conservatives claiming it undermined women's morals. Scandal plagued the contest in the 1930s, leading to a minimum age requirement of 18 and the addition of chaperones. Television made the event a household name in 1954, and more recently feminists have agitated about the pageant's exploitation of women. Today, pageant directors are trying to reverse the contest's growing reputation for cultural irrelevance. The 2000 pageant brought in the lowest television ratings in its history.

Lois Delander from Illinois was the proud winner of the 1927 Miss America title.

An emotional
Katie Harman
(Miss Oregon)
being crowned
Miss America
2002 by the
previous
year's winner,
Angela Perez.

A driver in New Orleans stands in front of his Coca-Cola delivery truck filled with the famously curvaceous glass bottles.

## 1929
## COCA-COLA

Coca-Cola was invented in 1886 by an Atlanta pharmacist as a "brain and nerve tonic." The drink was available at soda fountains and cost 5 cents a glass. It got its name from two ingredients in the original recipe—extracts of the kola nut and coca leaves. By 1903, the use of cocaine was controversial, and the company decided to use only spent coca leaves. The formula today does not include coca, but it does incorporate lime juice, orange, lemon, nutmeg, cinnamon, and coriander flavorings.

Coca-Cola did not become a worldwide brand until a strong network of bottlers was able to distribute the product across the country. A candy store owner in Mississippi was the first to put Coke in a bottle in 1894, and five years later a group of businessmen obtained exclusive rights to bottle the drink across the country. They paid $1 for the privilege. The famous bottle was invented in 1916 specifically for Coke by a glass company in Indiana, and it is one of the few packages ever granted trademark status by the United States patent office.

Since then, Coke has gone from being an American icon to a worldwide phenomenon. Coca-Cola is consumed 190 million times every day in more than 80 languages and in over 35 countries.

# CIVIL RIGHTS

Rosa Parks (right) riding on a newly integrated bus in Montgomery, Alabama, following the Supreme Court ruling that ended the successful 381-day boycott of segregated buses.

When Rosa Parks refused to give up her seat to a white passenger on a Montgomery, Alabama, bus on December 1, 1955, she set off a black boycott of the city's buses that eventually led to laws ending institutionalized segregation in the South. A new era of the civil rights movement was born.

Despite the fact that the majority of Montgomery's bus riders were black, they had to undergo humiliations such as paying the driver at the front of the bus, and then reboarding at the back, where they were required to sit in a separate section. They were not allowed to sit across from a white patron, and they were required to give up a seat if a white passenger was standing.

When the bus driver threatened to have Parks arrested for remaining seated, she quietly and firmly replied, "You may go on and do so." It eventually took the United States Supreme Court to end the bus boycott, by ruling that Alabama's segregation laws were unconstitutional. A little more than a year later, Rosa Parks rode on an integrated bus.

Parks received the Congressional Gold Medal of Honor in 1999, the highest award bestowed by the United States government, for "bringing America home to our founders' dream." Her example of the power of an individual to effect enormous change is the cornerstone of America, and her dignity and modesty under fire are an inspiration to all.

Rosa Parks was given a standing ovation in Washington, D.C., when she received the Congressional Gold Medal of Honor.

## HOT DOGS

Variously known as frankfurters, franks, weenies, weiner, red hots, and dogs, hot dogs have been eaten in the United States since European immigrants brought them to the country in the 19th century. Charles Feltman is credited with popularizing them when he opened up a hot dog stand on Coney Island in 1871. He sold 3,684 hot dogs during his first year of business.

By 1893, hot dogs had become standard fare at baseball games, a tradition started by a German immigrant who owned the St Louis Browns. During major league seasons today, fans eat 26 million hot dogs. Babe Ruth once ate 12 dogs between games in a double header, and had to be rushed to the hospital.

Historians are not sure whether the name hot dog came from the food's resemblance to German dachshund dogs or a sarcastic comment on the origins of the meat. Today, hot dogs are made from beef or a combination of pork and beef. Americans consume an average of 60 per year, most between Memorial Day and Labor Day.

A New York City hot dog vendor stands beside his cart. He also sells that other great American favorite—lemonade.

A hot dog vendor on Bourbon Street in New Orleans, Louisiana—with an umbrella and a fancy cart, nothing much has changed over the years with this American classic.

# 1930

## SCHOOL BUSES

State-run school transportation systems date back to 1869. They quickly became commonplace and, by 1919, every state in the country had one.

The yellow school bus has replaced the little red schoolhouse as the enduring symbol of education in America. Nearly 55 percent of students in kindergarten through 12th grade ride a bus to school every day—that's over 10 billion rides a year.

In 1869, Massachusetts was the first state to begin a pupil transportation system, and by 1919 all 48 states had them. The color yellow was chosen for school buses in 1939, the same year that the first minimum safety standards were adopted. School buses do not have to be yellow, but the National Highway Traffic Safety Administration recommends yellow so that motorists know that children are inside. Other safety standards include energy-absorbing seats, stop arms, and improved emergency exits and rearview mirrors.

Yellow is the recommended color for school buses so that motorists are alerted to the fact that children are on board.

Boys in Decatur, Illinois, selling lemonade to raise money to give the local zoo's bear population a new home.

# LEMONADE STANDS

Legend has it that lemonade was invented in France in the 17th century, but most Americans had not tasted it until irrigation turned Florida and California into lemon-growing states. How it became the drink of choice for entrepreneurial youngsters is anyone's guess.

Lemonade stands have become an American institution, and are usually seen on warm days when school is closed. Teachers even use the concept of lemonade stands to teach math, and "Lemonade Stand" is now a popular computer game where the object is to make a profit.

Most people like lemonade, however, because it tastes good. Although mixes abound, making fresh lemonade is tricky. The amount of sugar is critical—too little can lead to mouth puckering tartness, and too much will fail to quench the thirst. Most commercially grown lemons are lightly waxed after being picked to preserve moisture, so it is essential to remove the wax if the recipe requires the use of whole lemons.

A lemonade stand in Coeur d'Alene, Idaho—selling this refreshing drink continues to be a favourite entrepreneurial activity for America's children.

# sports & entertainment

John McEnroe in action at Wimbledon in 1981—he beat Björn Borg to win the championship.

John McEnroe, the number one tennis player in the world from 1981 to 1984, was as famous for his temper as he was for his shot-making. During a match leading up to the Wimbledon final in 1981, which he won against Björn Borg, he was fined $1,500 for calling an umpire "the pits of the world." He was suspended from the game for two months in 1987 after the U.S. Open, where he was fined for misconduct and verbal abuse. His frequent on-court tantrums earned him the nickname "Superbrat."

Known for his serve-and-volley tactics, his footwork, and tremendous eye-hand coordination, no one disputed McEnroe's abilities as a tennis player. He won three Wimbledon championships, four U.S. Open titles, 17 Grand Slam championships, and he helped the United States win five Davis Cups. He retired from the tour in 1992.

As a young man, McEnroe's temper cost him fans as well as endorsements, but now he enjoys a thriving career in the media, having worked as a commentator for the CBS, NBC, and USA networks. McEnroe seems to have gained some equanimity with age, and it suits him.

Having retired from the tour in 1992, a more sedate McEnroe now commentates on the game for television.

A smartly dressed couple on a bicycle for two in front of the White House, Washington, D.C. As the bicycle grew in popularity, the corset and bustle fell out of fashion.

The image of the surfer as a young bronzed god made the sport extremely popular in the 1920s and 1930s.

## SURFING 1929

When Captain Cook and his men arrived in Hawaii in 1778, surfing was deeply ingrained into Hawaiian culture and religion. Kings and commoners alike rode the waves, although society was highly stratified, and each had their own beaches. Within 50 years, however, Europeans had changed Hawaii forever, with new technologies, languages, diseases, and gods. Surfing fell into decline, stripped of its sacred aspects and cultural heritage.

It did not begin to revive until 1907, when Jack London published a story on surfing in *The Lady's Home Companion* after a visit to Hawaii. That same year, a Hawaiian named George Freeth, whom London described as "a young god bronzed with sunburn," gave a surfing demonstration in California, and the sport came to the United States. In the 1920s and 1930s, beach parties with surfing and fresh lobster pulled from the ocean were taking place up and down the pristine California coast.

By the 1960s, with help from the movie *Gidget*, surfing had become part of mainstream America. Relatively heavy balsa and redwood surfboards gradually gave way to lighter, shorter boards made from a variety of materials. The latest breakthrough is tow-in surfing, when surfers are towed like skiers behind jet skis, which then "slingshot" them out on to the wave faces.

Today, jet skis are sometimes used to tow surfers into the water and propel them on to the faces of the waves.

# BOXING 1975

Muhammad Ali admiring his reflection for the cameras. Declaring how much prettier he was than his opponents—because he was a better boxer and did not get hit as much—was a favorite pre-match taunt.

Laila Ali has a hard act to follow. The second youngest of Muhammad Ali's nine children, she took up professional boxing when she was 21, after seeing the Women's Heavyweight Champion fight on television in 1998. Although some say she is cashing in on her father's fame, her fierce commitment to training and her strong record suggest otherwise.

Perhaps she inherited her discipline from her father, known for his spartan lifestyle. He won the World Heavyweight Championship title from Sonny Liston in a legendary fight in 1964, and knocked him out in the first round during a rematch in Maine in 1965. Between 1965 and 1967, he successfully defended his title nine times. A fearless self-promoter, he became famous for phrases like "I am the greatest" and "Float like a butterfly, sting like a bee."

However, Ali was more than a famous fighter. Inspired by the black-rights activist Malcolm X, he adopted the Muslim faith and changed his name from Cassius Clay to Muhammad Ali. In 1967, he declared himself a conscientious objector to the Vietnam War and refused induction into the U.S. Army. Ali was stripped of his title and barred from the ring. He regained the title in 1974 from Joe Frazier.

Ali announced he had Parkinson's disease in 1984, but despite his failing health, he remains a hero. His belief in his principles, his stunning athleticism, and his joyous hucksterism appeal to people everywhere.

Ali's daughter Laila has also become a successful boxer.

People watch with fascination as elephants from the Ringling Brothers Circus line up in a train yard.

P. T. Barnum founded his Grand and Traveling Circus, Menagerie, and Caravan in 1870, at a time when professional entertainment was a rare treat for people living on farms and in small towns. From the start, the show included a variety of wild animals, but it is the elephants that have always been the most beloved.

Jumbo is perhaps the most famous elephant of all. When he arrived in New York City in 1882, thousands were on the docks waiting to greet him. Over the next three years, before he died, he was the focal point of the show and was seen by an estimated 2 million people. His name came to be synonymous with the word "big."

Today, people are still amazed by the delicacy and sensitivity of elephants, who weigh seven or eight tons yet can balance on a barrel. In fact, love of these creatures has spawned controversy over whether circuses treat them humanely. Some people believe that elephants are wild animals and should be freed from their role as entertainers.

Ringling Brothers and Barnum and Bailey Circus elephants performing a routine at a show in Los Angeles, California.

Going to see a double-feature at the local drive-in movie theater reached the peak of its popularity in the 1950s.

DRIVE-IN

GREGORY PECK & ANNE BAXTER
YELLOW SKY
MY LITTLE CHICKADEE
MAE WEST & W C FIELDS

**1951**

## DRIVE-IN THEATERS

Before VCRs and cable television, there were drive-in movie theaters. Now, in these days of homes with private screening rooms, drive-in theaters seem quaint. However, 70 years ago, they were the only place you could watch a double-feature, eat, drink, and talk about the movie with your best friend without bothering anyone.

The first drive-in opened on June 6, 1933, in Camden, New Jersey, and showed the movie *Wife Beware*. After World War II, drive-ins started hosting "open houses" during the day to acquaint people with where to park, how the sound systems worked, and what food was available. By the 1950s, the drive-in boom was underway, with the number of theaters growing from less than 1,000 in 1948 to close to 5,000 by 1958. Some theaters could accommodate up to 3,000 cars, and the larger theaters added miniature trains, pony rides, boat rides, miniature golf, and even talent shows. The gates would open as much as three hours before the movie started.

By the 1980s, however, drive-ins were becoming a relic. The land they occupied was often too valuable to be used only at night, and soon shopping malls and multiplex cinemas replaced them. Some 800 drive-ins exist today, and going to one is more a novelty than a commonplace experience.

Compared to the 1950s and 1960s, there are few drive-in movie theaters in existence today, although some, such as the Fiesta in Carlsbad, New Mexico, are making a comeback.

The junior ice hockey team players from Lake Placid Elementary School, New York, diving for the puck during a match.

Ice hockey as we know it began in Canada in the 1850s, but its origins were with Canadian Indians, who as early as the 1740s were found playing a similar game. They called it "Baggataway." In summer, they played it on the plains, and in winter they moved to frozen lakes and ponds. Some think that our word hockey came from a cry they yelled while playing, which sounded like "ho ee."

By 1890, hockey had spread to the United States, and in 1917 the National Hockey League (NHL) was formed with teams from both Canada and the U.S. Formerly dominated by Canadian players, a growing number of U.S. and European skaters are now appearing. Although the U.S. team won the Olympic gold medal both in 1960 at Squaw Valley, and in 1980, at Lake Placid, they were not able to repeat the performance in 2002 at Salt Lake City, where the Canadian team claimed the gold after beating the U.S. 5–2.

A fiercely fought match between the Colorado Avalanches and the St Louis Blues.

# MINIATURE GOLF

In the 1930s miniature golf was regarded as both a legitimate sport and an enjoyable pastime.

Although miniature golf has been around since the turn of the 20th century, it gained popularity in the 1930s as a legitimate sport—an inexpensive, condensed version of the real thing. People liked it because everyone could play it, pros and whackers alike.

Since then, however, putt-putt has developed a reputation as more of a kitsch game for klutzes than a serious athletic competition. On roadsides across America, mini-golf courses combine architectural details in illogical combinations—usually, fortunately, miniaturized. It is still possible on courses constructed in the 1950s to see dinosaurs mixed with pyramids, and octopuses splayed across Arabian palaces. For some reason, windmills are popular, as are gnomes.

Today, a new breed of super-landscaped, million-dollar mini-golf courses are making their debut. No longer dominated by Mom and Pop operators, the new courses are seeking to please a generation of Disneyland-goers for whom bigger is better. Gushing waterfalls and mountainous terrain have replaced tacky figurines, but the game remains the same.

Miniature golf courses such as this one in Wisconsin are much more sophisticated than in the past.

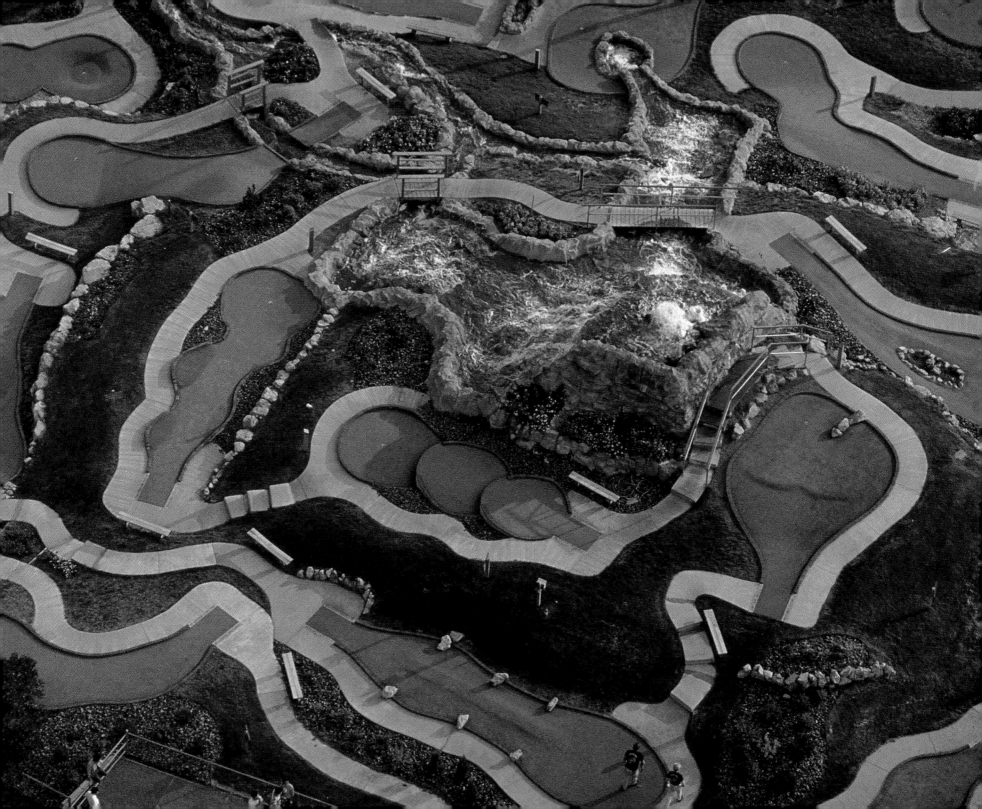

RODEO **1933**

Earl Thode riding Tumble Weed, a bucking bronco, for the required 10 seconds to win the special award during the 8th annual rodeo given by cowboy actor Hoot Gibson at his ranch in Saugus, California.

Rodeos have come a long way from their origins as simple cattle roundups. When the West was still young, riding and roping were part of everyday life on the ranch, and rodeos evolved as a way for cowboys to win bragging rights. They were a chance for a cowhand to show off his skills breaking a tough bronco or roping a runaway steer.

However, just as the West was becoming tame and cowboy skills were becoming less important, "Buffalo Bill" Cody started his Wild West Show in 1882. He included roping, riding, bronco busting, and bull riding. The success of this show, which toured the country for years, spurred the growth of rodeo across the United States. By 1890, rodeos were common across the West.

Today's rodeos barely resemble those of the early days—they are more an entertaining show than a display of working skills. Performers compete in over 80 rodeos a year, and often spend over 200 days annually on the road, traveling from show to show.

A cowboy roping a calf during a rodeo. Modern rodeos are popular entertainment shows and fiercely competitive.

A group "nature sliding" in Mount Rainier National Park, Washington. The seats of the "tin trousers" they are wearing are paraffined to reduce friction.

# SNOW SPORTS

Heavy snowfall lies over Mount Rainier National Park in Washington for about nine months every year—perfect conditions for intrepid adventurers. In 1912, Olive Rand was the first person to ski on Mount Rainier, using makeshift wooden boards. She was on an outing sponsored by the Tacoma Mountaineers, a club that brought hundreds of visitors to the park even in the cold winter months. For those without skis, the club also sponsored "nature sliding" down giant snow fields. So-called tin trousers were worn, because they had paraffin on the seats to reduce friction.

Snow sports have changed quite a bit since then. Early adventurers and their makeshift equipment inspired Jake Burton Carpenter to shape the first snowboards out of wood in 1970. He used rubber straps for bindings. In the past decade, the number of people snowboarding has jumped from 1 million to 12 million. Today, there are snowboard parks in almost every ski area, including at Crystal Mountain, adjacent to Mount Ranier.

A snowboarder in Wyoming displays one of the many athletic maneuvers that can be performed.

## FOOTBALL 1935

Although colleges have been organizing football games since 1869, the game back then was more similar to rugby and soccer than football as we know it today. The first set of rules was formed by representatives from Columbia, Rutgers, Princeton, and Yale—tackling below the waist was legalized, downs were invented, and the number of players was reduced from 15 to 11.

Despite the Rules Committee, the game was becoming increasingly dangerous for players. Brutal mass plays resulted in 18 deaths, and 180 players suffered serious injuries. President Theodore Roosevelt asked for intervention, and in 1905 the Rules Committee established what would later be known as the National Collegiate Athletic Association, or NCAA. They prohibited mass plays and legalized the forward pass. By the 1920s, football was the second favorite sport of Americans, after baseball.

Now, of course, it is America's favorite sport. Collegiate football is thriving, and often serves as a stepping stone to professional football. A game once only enjoyed by sideline enthusiasts now commands millions of television viewers weekly.

Football players for Boston and Geneva colleges compete for the ball during a game played in Boston.

A Boston College running back slips through Syracuse University defenders during a game in Boston.

## BEACH VOLLEYBALL

Two young women enjoy a friendly game of beach volleyball in Lincoln, Nebraska.

Volleyball was originally invented in 1895 by an instructor at the YMCA in Holyoke, Massachusetts, for wimps who wanted a less physically aggressive sport than basketball. Today, beach volleyball attracts crowds eager for a glimpse of bronzed athletes in tiny bathing suits who dive across blazing sand to spike the ball over the net.

An incident at the 2000 Summer Olympics in Sydney, Australia, helps to explain the growing popularity of the sport. When an injury forced the Mexican men's beach volleyball team out of the match, the enterprising American team cobbled together an unofficial game with an NBC sports announcer and the remaining uninjured Mexican—just for the fun of it. The crowd's enthusiasm was as much a celebration of beach culture as it was of the game itself. Kevin Wong, one of the American players, said afterwards: "At the essence of our sport, it's just four guys going out on a beach with a ball."

Although the first two-man beach volleyball tournament was held in 1948 in California, it was not until 1996 that two-person beach volleyball was added to the Olympics. Its blatant promotion of audience entertainment has made some Olympic officials blanch, but the crowds love it. Whether players are competing for an Olympic gold medal or just having fun on a summer day at the beach, the combination of sun, sand, skimpy suits, and sport is hard to beat.

Athletic moves and skimpy suits combined with sun and sand make beach volleyball a great sport to watch as well as play.

# SAILING

Sailing has come a long way from its beginnings as a means of transportation. The Dutch began the transformation of sailing into a sport in the 17th century, when they made sleek and fast *jaghtschiffs* to run down pirates. The English picked it up, changing the word to yacht along the way, and passed it to American colonists.

The oldest yacht club in the United States is the New York Yacht Club (NYYC), founded in 1844. In 1851 NYYC members raced against British sailors around the Isle of Wight, and the trophy became known as the America's Cup. Now the most prestigious event in international sailboat racing, every America's Cup race was won by the U.S. until recently, when Australia and New Zealand were victorious.

Traditionally a sport for the wealthy, new methods of boat building have made sailing less expensive. Perhaps the biggest barrier to becoming a true sailor is learning the language. There are "blue widows" (wives left at home while their husbands sail), "coffee grinders" (winches), and then there is getting "bilged," "slewed," or "three sheets to the wind" (drunk).

A yacht sailing off New York City with its sails at full mast.

Sailboats on the Charles River in Boston, Massachusetts. New innovations in boat building have made sailing a much more affordable activity.

# LITTLE LEAGUE

Little League baseball is a springtime ritual played on 12,000 fields across the U.S. and in 103 other countries around the world. Although football has replaced baseball as America's favorite sport, for children and their parents baseball still rules—over 4 million kids and coaches participate every year.

It all began in Williamsport, Pennsylvania, in 1938, when Carl Stotz realized his nephews were too young to play organized baseball. Stotz and two neighbors, George and Bert Bebble, created a three-team league, and after being turned down by 56 businesses, they managed to convince a lumber company, a dairy, and a pretzel maker to sponsor the teams. In June 1939, the first Little League pitch was thrown.

Despite the wholesomeness, the sport is not without controversy. Maria Pepe was a pitcher for three games on her Hoboken, New Jersey, team in the early 1970s before angry parents stepped in to protest that she was a girl. Little League headquarters threw her off the team, but in 1974 the New Jersey Superior Court ruled that both boys and girls, ages 8 through 12, be allowed to play. In 2001, a Bronx, New York, team was stripped of its third-place finish in the Little League World Series after it was discovered that the team's star pitcher was too old to play. Danny Almonte, the first player to pitch a perfect World Series game in 44 years, was 14 years old.

A player tries to reach first base before the ball during a Little League game in Williamsport, Pennsylvania.

Little Leaguers standing for the Pledge of Allegiance during the opening ceremony of the season in Pittsburgh, Pennsylvania.

# THE INDY 500

A view of the stands and track at the Indianapolis Speedway during the annual Memorial Day 500-mile race.

Few sporting events have as many traditions as the Indianapolis 500. Considered by many Americans to be the greatest event in racing, drivers have been competing in the Indy 500 since 1911. The first winner, Ray Harroun, completed the 200 laps around the 2½ mile oval track at an average speed of 74 miles per hour. More recently, in 1986, Bobby Rahal completed the 500 miles at an average speed of 170 miles per hour. Two women qualified for the race for the first time in 2000— unfortunately, they crashed out together.

Despite changing times, traditions at the Indy 500 hold fast. One of the oldest is the sounding of a percussion bomb at 5 a.m. on the day of the race. This custom is thought to date back to the earliest years, when the bomb was detonated to alert fans that the Speedway gates had opened. In 1946, the song "Back Home in Indiana" was performed right before the green start flag was dropped, and it has been a part of the celebration every year since then. Thousands of multicolored balloons are released at the same time.

Perhaps the most unusual tradition is when the champion celebrates by drinking from an old-fashioned glass quart of milk at the victory ceremony. Louis Meyer started that in 1936, when he guzzled a bottle of buttermilk because his mother told him that it would refresh him.

Modern racing cars can reach more than double the speed attained by the first winner of the Indy 500.

An excited young boy at a bowling alley in Springfield, Vermont—a picture of wholesome family fun.

## BOWLING 1962

Bowling, a particularly clean-cut sport today, has not always been so—in fact, the state of Connecticut outlawed ninepins in 1841 because it was a favorite with gamblers. The story goes that a tenth pin was added to get around the Connecticut ban, but it has never been proven.

Regardless of its lack of respectability, bowling was extremely popular in the late 1800s, particularly in New York City. German immigrants brought it to Chicago, Cincinnati, Detroit, St Louis, and Milwaukee. By the turn of the 20th century, rules and equipment were standardized, and the first National Bowling Championships was held in Chicago. Gambling was eliminated, and soon women were playing, too.

Today, some 60 million people in the United States bowl at least once a year, and 7 million compete in league-sanctioned play. The Professional Bowlers Association was founded in 1958, and hosts about 40 tournaments each year.

Bowling continues to be popular throughout the United States, with around 60 million people playing at least once a year.

# CHEERLEADING

University of Maryland football cheerleaders raise a shout for their team.

What do Dwight Eisenhower, Franklin D. Roosevelt, Ronald Reagan, and George W. Bush have in common? All were once cheerleaders. This fast-growing activity had its birth at a University of Minnesota football game in 1898, where the pep club led the onlookers in yells from the stands. One young man got so excited that he jumped out in front of the bleachers, and cheerleading was born.

Men initially dominated cheerleading, but women became active in the 1920s. When soldiers returned home after World War II, the sexes began to collaborate, incorporating dancing, gymnastic, and partner routines. The Dallas Cowboys Cheerleaders added Broadway-style dancing to their shows, but the squad did not become legendary until 1976 when a Super Bowl television camera caught one Cowboys cheerleader winking.

In the 1980s, cheerleading was recognized as a sport. Collegiate, high school, and even junior high school cheerleading competitions were established, with universal standards and safety guidelines. After a hiatus, male cheerleaders are once again joining the ranks, and moves are becoming more sophisticated, requiring greater coordination and strength. Trained to be smiling and optimistic, cheerleaders are asked to be exemplars of high spirits and good citizenship. Perhaps it was this training that helped the cheerleader presidents get prepared for the job.

The San Diego Chargers cheerleaders perform during a game against the Pittsburgh Steelers at Qualcomm Stadium in San Diego, California.

# the great outdoors

## ROOSEVELT DAM 1911

The lush lawns and verdant gardens in Phoenix, Arizona, would be unthinkable without the water supplies created by the Roosevelt Dam. In fact, Arizona itself only became a state in 1912, the year after the dam was completed—in part because the water from the dam allowed large-scale development of agriculture and industry on land that was formerly desert.

Roosevelt Dam was named after President Theodore Roosevelt, who was instrumental in approval of the Federal Reclamation Act of 1902. The act authorized western irrigation projects paid for by the federal government, and in 1911 Roosevelt Dam was the first completed dam. The original 280-foot wall was higher than Niagara Falls, and was built from huge, irregular stones hewn from nearby hillsides. The workforce consisted of a variety of ethnic groups—Apaches built roadways, African-Americans worked in the quarries, and Italian stonemasons installed the granite.

In 1996, Roosevelt Dam's distinctive stones were covered with smooth concrete and the height was raised by 77 feet to expand the reservoir's water storage and reduce the chance of flooding. The dam is now expected to accommodate Phoenix's water needs throughout the 21st century.

Theodore Roosevelt speaking at the dedication ceremony for the dam.

The Roosevelt Dam provides water and power for the city of Phoenix.

# GRAND CANYON

One of the seven natural wonders of the world, Grand Canyon is neither the deepest canyon nor the biggest, yet its tremendous vistas and brilliantly colored walls draw over 5 million visitors a year.

Although Native Americans populated the area on and off for centuries, the canyon remained largely unknown until Civil War veteran John Wesley Powell led a famous boat expedition through it in 1869. The one-armed geologist guided a party of nine men on the 1,000-mile journey down the Colorado River in four small wooden boats. After a second journey in 1872, he chose the name Grand Canyon.

By the turn of the 20th century, miners had abandoned their hopes of extracting lucrative minerals from the canyon, and tourism loomed as the major industry in the area. Fortunately, conservationists fought for the establishment of protected recreational areas, and in 1919 Grand Canyon became a national park.

Grand Canyon gets its beauty from its rocks, some of which are up to two billion years old. The exposed rock in the walls is much older than the canyon itself, which is only five to six million years old. Grand Canyon was formed by erosion caused by the Colorado River, as well as running water from rain, snowmelt, and tributary streams. The vivid colors in the layers are due to minerals, which impart subtle shades of red, yellow, and green to the canyon walls and corridors.

A view of the Grand Canyon from the south rim.

The spectacular canyon attracts over 5 million visitors each year from around the world.

The sculpting of Mount Rushmore was as much an engineering feat as an artistic one.

# MOUNT RUSHMORE

Those not lucky enough to have visited Mount Rushmore in South Dakota can see it immortalized in Alfred Hitchcock's classic movie *North by Northwest*. One of the movie's most thrilling sequences is a chase scene over the face of the monument, which becomes surreal because of the juxtaposition of humans against the larger-than-life features of four past American presidents.

The monument was the idea of the superintendent of the South Dakota state historical society. When work began on Mount Rushmore in 1927, it was the first time a sculpture of this magnitude had been attempted. Sculptor Gutzon Borglum directed his men to build a 506-step stairway with 45 ramps up the face of the mountain—the equivalent of a 40-story building. Up top, men were fitted into leather harnesses and lowered down the face of the granite by men above operating winches. After careful measurement, they painted instructions on the rock about where drilling should occur. Dynamite was stuffed into drill holes to blast the rock into general shape, and then drillers and carvers removed the rest of the stone.

Mount Rushmore National Memorial opened in 1941, and has remained popular ever since. In 1998, a Hall of Records containing documents that explain the meaning of the sculpted heads was dedicated and sealed so that future archeologists would have no doubt as to why Mount Rushmore is there.

The Mount Rushmore National Memorial features the heads of four American presidents: George Washington; Thomas Jefferson; Theodore Roosevelt and Abraham Lincoln.

A church in Taos Pueblo, New Mexico. Catholic churches were built in the area from the 16th century onward, when the Spanish conquered New Mexico and ordered the native Pueblo population to convert to Catholicism.

Religious conviction played an important role in the European settlement of New Mexico. It was inhabited by the ancestors of the Pueblo Indians when Spain conquered the area in 1521, and even the first Spanish expedition into what is now New Mexico in 1540 was as much about missionary zeal as it was about exploration.

By 1583, the Spanish king issued a royal law ordering that Indians convert to the Catholic faith. Franciscan friars established missions, forced the Indians to work for the Church, and outlawed the Pueblo religion. There were several Pueblo revolts in the 17th century, but by the 18th century the Spanish and Pueblo peoples had established peace.

It has been estimated that 88 percent of the state's population was Catholic when New Mexico became a state in 1912. Today, although the religious makeup of the state is much more diverse, the many old Catholic churches are a reminder of New Mexico's heritage.

A group of native New Mexicans at one of the many beautiful white churches to be found in the area.

# 1942
## SNAKE RIVER

Photographers at the beginning of the 20th century in America were instrumental in convincing Congress to protect the seemingly boundless wilderness by creating national parks. Increasing settlement and industrialization were threatening the West's natural beauty, and preservation of the land became a driving force behind many photographers' works.

Ansel Adams, one of several noted photographers of the period, became an active proponent of conservation. He made his first trip at age 14 to Yosemite National Park, which he photographed with his first camera, a Kodak #1 Box Brownie. The trip started his love affair with the West, and he returned there nearly every year of his life to capture rivers, mountains, moonrises, and all manner of natural wonders. As a member of the Sierra Club's board of directors, he successfully lobbied Congress to create a new national park in Kings River Canyon, California.

The Snake River flows through Grand Teton National Park, which was designated a national park in 1950. Nearly 3 million visitors come to the park every year, many of who float on the Snake River for its scenic views.

Photographer Ansel Adams captures the beauty of Snake River and the surrounding countryside.

Fly fishers on the Snake River in Grand Teton National Park, Wyoming.

# 1980
## MOUNT ST HELENS

The eruption of Mount St Helens in southwest Washington on May 18, 1980, changed thousands of peoples' lives and turned over 200 square miles into a gray wasteland. The largest landslide in recorded history swept down the mountain at speeds up to 150 miles per hour. Huge mudflows destroyed 27 bridges, 200 homes, and 185 miles of roads. A massive ash cloud grew to 80,000 feet in fifteen minutes, and reached the East Coast in three days. Fifty-seven people were killed.

The blast region today still looks like a moonscape—gray with volcanic ash and mostly barren. However, plants and animals are now returning to the area. Some, like gophers, mice, and other diggers, were able to survive the eruption by going underground. Wildlife such as coyotes and elk live on the edge of the blast zone but routinely travel through it, leaving waste products filled with seeds that germinate easily in the fertile volcanic soil.

Mount St Helens is expected to erupt again, but no one knows when. In the meantime, wisps of steam are constantly vented, and minor earthquakes have become more frequent. Every day, 100 hikers are allowed to climb to the crater rim, where they have a view of the crater itself, as well as nearby volcanoes such as Mt Rainier and Mt Hood.

A deadly plume of smoke and ash erupting from Mount St Helens.

Nine years after the eruption of Mount St Helens, fir trees began to grow in a forest devastated by the volcano.

A couple enjoy an *al fresco* twilight dinner with friends in the shadow of their trailer in Antelope Valley, Utah.

## TRAILER HOMES 1939

The first trailer homes were built in 1926 to serve finicky "campers" who did not want to brave the elements. They preferred to set up camp with a traveling roof over their heads.

In 1943, trailers averaged about 8 feet in width and 20 feet in length. They had three or four separate sleeping sections, but no bathrooms. After World War II, the trailers evolved into mobile homes to provide cheap housing for veterans and their families.

By 1948, trailers had grown to 30 feet in length, and bathrooms were introduced. Over the years, they continued to expand (try passing a doublewide trailer on the highway) and modern appliances were incorporated. Mobile homes officially became "manufactured housing" in 1976, when federal regulations mandating strict building guidelines took effect.

Meanwhile, people continue to love the idea of driving through the woods towing all the comforts of home to a campsite. Camping trailers now have amenities including pop tents, electricity, and fold-out tables.

Early motor homes such as this one (left) provided mobility and comfort on camping trips, but were soon put to use as permanent accommodation after World War II.

## BEARS 1905

Black bears are found nowhere else in the world except North America. They used to roam the entire continent, from the tip of Alaska to Mexico, but now they are extinct in about 15 of the states they originally inhabited. Although they have lost territory, there are more black bears today than when European settlers arrived. Then there were about 500,000 black bears roaming the continent; now there are closer to 700,000.

Despite the thriving population, people are hard at work ensuring the preservation of bears' habitats. Grizzly bears, the black bear's less friendly relation, are considered a threatened species in the lower 48 states, meaning that they are likely to become endangered. An intensive bear management program was begun at Yellowstone Park in 1970, with the purpose of restoring the park's natural populations of grizzly and black bears.

Black bear hunting is currently allowed in 25 states, although it engenders mixed feelings. In Minnesota, where the state estimates that the bear population has quadrupled during the last 20 years, hunters were allowed in 2001 to kill two bears with each license in an effort to reduce the growing numbers.

Four hunters pose with the body of a black bear draped over a boulder at Lake Chelan, Washington.

Although the population of black bears is thriving, grizzly bears are a threatened species in 48 states.

Cowboys eating at a chuck tent during a roundup. Hearty foods were served, including stewed meat, beans, freshly baked biscuits, and gallons of strong black coffee.

# COWBOYS 1905

That most famous of American icons, the rugged cowboy, still exists today, but his fame comes from a brief period starting in the mid-19th century. By that time, settlers in the southwest had established ranches, taking advantage of wild long-horned cattle originally brought by Spanish colonists and vast grasslands perfect for grazing.

However, it was not until after the Civil War that cowboys became a breed apart. The war-ravaged eastern United States desperately needed beef, which was plentiful in the west. Ranchers, hearing opportunity knock, looked for ways to get their cattle to eastern markets.

Cowboys were hired to drive huge herds of cattle north to railroad depots, often for distances as long as 1,000 miles. The cowboy's life was rugged. Typically between 14 and 18 years old, a cowboy spent 10 hours every day on horseback, and slept under the stars with his saddle as a pillow. Meals were provided by a cook from a trail kitchen built in the back of a chuck wagon or set up in a tent.

The end of the cowboy's era came at the turn of the 20th century, when railroads penetrated even the more inaccessible parts of the southwest and it became unnecessary to drive cattle hundreds of miles to market. Today, cowboys still drive cattle to and from their summer grazing range, but the distances are short and civilization is never far away.

A cowboy in Florida gives a young calf a horseback ride.

CHANDELIER TREE
UNDERWOOD PARK

## 1942
## REDWOOD TREES

California's giant redwood trees embody America's ongoing feud between capitalists and conservationists. The towering redwoods are the biggest trees in the world, and many of them were living well before Columbus found the New World. However, American entrepreneurs saw an opportunity they could not ignore—bore holes through the trunks and charge admission to allow vehicles to drive through.

The Chandelier Drive-Thru Tree Park in Leggett is one of several such attractions, which visitors find either charming or tacky, depending on their point of view. Estimated to be over 2,400 years old, the original drive-through tree is 315 feet tall and 21 feet in diameter. The hole was carved out in 1934 using a chisel and a crosscut saw. After World War II, it was enlarged for the new, larger cars, and a gift shop was built.

No tree, of course, is big enough to accommodate today's Winnebagos, and many tourists have to satisfy themselves with walking through the trunk. Modern environmentalists have made sure that no new drive-through trees are created, however, so the remaining few now have an exclusive franchise on the concept.

The giant redwood tree at Chandelier Drive-Thru Tree Park is 315 feet tall, 21 feet wide, and estimated to be over 2,400 years old.

Although the creation of drive-through trees is now prohibited, existing ones such as the Chandelier tree continue to attract visitors.

A team of loggers on an Idaho river engaged in the hazardous task of loosening a log jam and driving the logs downstream.

Loggers used to be an elite fraternity. They were pioneers who used their strength against the most abundant raw material the land once had to offer—wood. America, with its vast, lush forests, exported timber to Europe as early as 1607, and in the 1800s the Industrial Revolution caused a surge in demand for lumber to build businesses and homes.

To meet these growing needs, lumberjacks had to go deeper and deeper into the forests and develop better methods of cutting trees and moving the timber to market. October to March were the cutting and hauling months, after which came the annual spring drive. Early on, teams of oxen hauled logs to rivers, where they were floated to their destinations. By the beginning of the 20th century, however, railroads were built to carry the wood. At around the same time, lumberjacks began using crosscut saws to fell the trees instead of axes, increasing their efficiency.

The idea that forests could not provide an endless supply of timber for logging emerged in the United States in the 1920s, but efforts concentrated on setting aside forest to ensure a future supply of wood rather than conservation. By 1960, as consumer demand for wood products continued to escalate, environmentalists were demanding that forests be permanently protected. Logging today is almost completely mechanized, and now the debate centers on creating sustainable logging practices to ensure that there is something left for future generations.

Most of the logging process is now mechanized. Here, a tugboat pushes logs down Coeur d'Alene River near Harrison, Idaho.

# NIAGARA FALLS 1859

Attractive to both honeymooners and daredevils, as well as to the average tourist, Niagara Falls never ceases to amaze. Originally, as much as 5.5 billion gallons of water per hour flowed over the falls. Today, the amount is controlled by the U.S. and Canadian governments in order to slow erosion, which used to move the brink of the falls backward an estimated 3 feet every year. The falls are one of the largest sources of hydroelectric power in the United States.

The power and beauty of the water has compelled many daredevils over the years to try going over the falls. The first attempt, by a 62-year-old schoolteacher who claimed to be 43, was in 1901. Strapped into a barrel, she made the 170-foot plunge without mishap. Of the 15 people who have so far attempted the falls, 10 have survived.

The most amazing story is Roger Woodward's, who was swept over the brink after a boating accident in 1960 when he was seven years old. He was pulled from the water on to the *Maid of the Mist*, a tourist boat at the base of the falls, with only minor injuries, having survived without any protection at all.

Visitors overlooking Niagara Falls from Prospect Point on the U.S. bank.

The American and Canadian governments now control the quantity of water flowing over the falls in order to reduce erosion.

Inuits are the most sparsely distributed people in the world, with different groups inhabiting the northern reaches of the globe between Alaska and Greenland for an area spanning 3,200 miles. However, their manners and customs are remarkably uniform, despite the diffusion of the people and the encroachments of modern civilization.

The name Inuit, which means "the real people," was officially adopted in 1977 to replace the term Eskimo. In traditional Inuit culture, the family is the most important social group. Marriage, which is a virtual necessity for physical survival, is based on a strict division of labor, with men building houses and obtaining food, and women cooking and making clothing. There is no community legal structure, so disputes are settled using social means—ridicule, wrestling matches, or song duels, when the angered individuals extemporize insulting ditties.

Some changes have occurred, however. Western housing has replaced the igloo, processed foods are eaten instead of the traditional diet culled from the seas, and Christianity is replacing the Inuits' original religious beliefs, which centered on humankind's relations with animals and a hostile environment. The International Inuit Circumpolar Conference meets every three years to provide a forum for discussion of common problems and to lobby for preservation of the environment.

Wearing furs and fishing through a hole in the ice, this woman typifies the traditional image of an Inuit.

Although much of Inuit culture remains unchanged, modernizations have occurred. This Inuit man is using a snowmobile to collect supplies at a whale hunting camp in Barrow, Alaska.

# NATIVE AMERICANS 1962

There are more pow wows being held today by Native Americans than there were hundreds of years ago, when Europeans first came to this land. The tradition is ancient—dances were performed before warriors left the tribe to hunt, raid, or do battle, and there was also a celebration upon their return.

The modern pow wow emerged after the growth of reservations, when tribal customs and religions were outlawed. The grass dance, in which tribal elders would re-enact brave deeds, was one of the few ceremonies allowed. It became a key link to a vanishing past. Today, pow wows are usually presented by one tribe to welcome and honor Native Americans from other tribes, and the focus is on dance, song, and family celebration.

Some pow wows feature competition in dancing categories such as traditional, fancy, grass, shawl, and jingle-dress. A dancer's clothing, called regalia, is a prized possession. It is handmade by the dancer, and every article has some significance. When a new dancer comes out in regalia, it is cause for great celebration. Pow wows were traditionally held in the spring, but can now be found almost anytime throughout the United States.

A crowd of 30,000 watch over 250 dancers from 10 states in a pow wow near Starved Rock in Ottawa.

Dancers performing at the Seafair Indian Days Pow Wow at Discovery Park in Seattle.

A wagon train of American homesteaders moves across the open plains, migrating westward.

A truck transporting goods along Highway 84, which runs from Georgia to Colorado.

# ROAD TRIPS

Wagon trains were the pioneers' only way of moving westward before the transcontinental railroad was completed. As soon as proper roads were built in the east, people began hitching horses to Conestoga wagons to move themselves and their possessions from the coastal cities toward Ohio settlements.

The typical wagon train was developed on the plains and prairies of the Midwest. There, large groups traveled in covered wagons, banding together to survive the hardships of traveling vast distances and the danger from hostile Native Americans. Trains were highly organized, with participants signing a contract that laid out the terms of joining, the rules to be followed, and what officials would be elected. Sometimes both a military captain and a civilian leader were elected; at other times one man fulfilled both roles. Lieutenants were also chosen, and an order was established for the wagons both on and off the trail. At night, wagons drew around in a circular corral, and guards were posted to ward off attack.

Wagon trains disappeared in the later part of the 19th century, the victim of increasing settlement and diminishing threat from Native Americans. The need to be on the go remains, however, and road trips continue to be a favorite American pastime as well as a means of transporting goods and possessions.

# COTTON PICKING

Cotton pickers in Alabama. The work was hard, labor intensive, and poorly paid.

Cotton played an important role in America's development from a fledgling nation to an economic power. In the early 19th century, southern states became the biggest single supplier of cotton to thriving English textile mills. During the period from 1815 to 1860, the crop comprised more than half the total value of American domestic exports. Cotton cultivation became the basis of the one-crop, slave-labor economy of the Deep South, and a major cause of the Civil War. Many southerners believed Britain would come to their defense in the hopes of preserving their trading relationship.

After the war, with the end of slave labor and declining soil fertility, cotton farming moved farther west to states such as Texas, Mississippi, Arizona, and Louisiana. Until recently, the United States was the world's leading cotton producer and it is second now only to China. Cheap labor, once the driving force behind successful cotton-producing nations, is no longer as critical due to the widespread use of mechanical cultivating and harvesting.

Cotton harvesters in Lost Hills, California. The use of machines to pick cotton has substantially reduced the need for cheap labor.

Religion is part of everyday life in the Bible Belt. Here, a Christian message shares space with advertisements for fertilizer and orangeade in Greene County, Georgia.

The Bible Belt is a swath running through the South and parts of the Midwest. It hosts large numbers of fundamentalist Christians. Fundamentalists believe in the literal truth of the Bible. They divide the world into absolute good and absolute evil, claim possession of the divine truth, and relish in unmasking the enemy.

The South was not always as religious as it is today. In the 1600s and 1700s the northern colonies attracted more religious people because of the promise of freedom from persecution. This situation had changed by 1850 however, when the census showed that although the New England and southern states had about the same population, the number of churches and churchgoers in the South was almost double that in the North.

Fundamentalist Christians believe their lives are totally controlled by God, and they make no apologies for their politics or their behavior. Church services can be dramatic, with weeping, moaning, and speaking in tongues not uncommon.

A believer expresses his opinion of Satan at a Harvest Crusade gathering in Anaheim, California.

# THE AMISH

Two Amish children sit in the back of their parents' buggy near Manassas, Virginia.

154

The Amish fled Europe in the 1720s, rejecting the union of church and state there. They were attracted by William Penn's promise of religious tolerance, and settled primarily in Pennsylvania, Ohio, and Indiana. Today, there are over 130,000 Amish living a simple, agrarian lifestyle.

The Amish follow basic Christian teachings, but unlike most other religions, their faith is intertwined with their entire culture. Many Amish do not use modern conveniences, such as telephones, cars, radios, and televisions. Simple dark suits are worn by men, and women wear plain dresses with long sleeves, apron, and bonnet. Marriage is not allowed outside the faith, and children attend one-room schools through to the 8th grade only. By the age of 12, girls are taught to cook meals for large crews of Amish workers, and teenage boys know farm operations.

By isolating themselves from the outside world, the Amish maintain a close-knit community that emphasizes the importance of serving and respecting one other. Members rarely stray from the fold in word or deed, because they risk being shunned by other members of the group, including their spouse. Although increasing tourism continues to bring the outside world in, some Amish welcome the interest of others because it serves to decrease the cultural gap and increase public support for their way of life.

An Amish boy in Lancaster County, Pennsylvania.

the city

## 1865

## RICHMOND, VIRGINIA

A devastated
Richmond at
the end of the
Civil War.

The illuminated buildings of downtown Richmond reflected in the still waters of the James River at twilight.

Located on the James River, only 110 miles from the federal capital of Washington, D.C., Richmond, Virginia, was a symbol of the South's secession from the Union from 1861 to 1865. Richmond, the capital city of the Confederate States of America, was a prime psychological target throughout the Civil War.

The city did not fall until April 2, 1865, when Union troops took over Petersburg 25 miles to the south. Confederate President Jefferson Davis abandoned the capital late that night. Richmond burned, as fires set by fleeing Confederates and looters raged out of control. The Confederate Army surrendered just seven days later.

The reconstruction period following the Civil War was a time of crisis. Richmond was slowly rebuilt, but it took longer to come to terms with a new way of life. Although the federal government passed civil rights legislation trying to secure basic rights for former slaves, it took another century for the United States to begin to live up to the promise of equality for all races. A milestone was achieved in 1990, when Lawrence Douglas Wilder was elected Governor of Virginia, the first African-American governor in U.S. history.

## CHICAGO 1925

Situated on the shore of Lake Michigan, Chicago boasts a beach that attracts crowds of bathers— luckily, it's not always windy.

Situated on a plain on the shore of Lake Michigan, Chicago did not get its nickname of the "Windy City" because of the weather. The title was coined in 1893 by *New York Sun* editor Charles Dana, who was tired of hearing long-winded politicians boasting about the World's Columbian Exposition held in Chicago that year.

However, in addition to being home to Wrigley's Spearmint Gum and the first steel-frame skyscraper, Chicago is the recipient of frequently changeable weather and high winds. In winter, frigid air sweeps into Chicago from the flat Great Plains. In the summer, when the lake is colder than the land, a breeze can make daytime temperatures at the beach 10°F lower than inland. If the breeze is strong, the entire city can be cooled.

Residents and office workers alike flock to the lakefront park that hugs the shoreline in downtown Chicago. Overlooked by the 100-story John Hancock building, activities there include volleyball, jogging, and biking.

Whether you prefer to stroll along the walkway or simply lie back and read, the beach is one of Chicago's most popular attractions.

A view of storefronts on the 420 block of Lenox Avenue in Harlem, New York City.

Harlem, the area of New York City north of 96th Street, was originally a place of rich country estates and farmland. When the elevated train service began running to Harlem in the 1880s, the area became solidly middle class and white. However, at the turn of the 20th century a land boom in Harlem resulted in overbuilding and high rents, and by 1904 landlords found they had empty apartments. Reluctantly, they began renting to African-American tenants, who for the first time had access to decent, attractive housing. By 1930, two-thirds of New York's black population lived there, and Harlem became the nation's first African-American city.

After World War I, Harlem was home for an artistic and intellectual ferment that profoundly influenced American culture. The Apollo Theater on 125th Street is famous for hosting every great jazz musician. Marcus Garvey, Malcolm X, Jesse Jackson, and Al Sharpton all centered their activism on Harlem.

Afflicted by the Depression and a variety of social ills, Harlem's fortunes waned after World War II. Now, however, it is experiencing a surge of interest, with a huge new shopping and movie complex being built on 125th Street and former President Bill Clinton renting offices there as well.

The Apollo Theater on 125th Street has played host to every great jazz musician.

Baltimore's oyster fleet during its peak—it harvested 15 million bushels of oysters in a single year.

Oysters in Baltimore's Chesapeake Bay in 1650 were huge—as big around as dinner plates. The colonists' appetites took their toll early on, and by 1700 oysters were being harvested when they were younger and about half that size. Baltimore did not begin commercial oystering until the early 1800s, when oyster beds in New England and New York were nearly depleted.

By the late 19th century, Baltimore was a city built on oysters. The Inner Harbor was a cannery row where people in packing plants shucked, steamed, and canned the bivalves. The harvest peaked in 1885, when 15 million bushels of oysters were pulled from the bay. Watermen were allowed to dredge for oysters in small, inexpensive sailboats called skipjacks, and mechanized tongs also increased production. All of these "improvements," however, resulted in the depletion of the oyster beds. When disease struck in the 1950s, the beds were almost destroyed.

Concern escalated when environmentalists proved that the ability of oysters to filter water played a critical role in keeping the bay clean. Today, oyster beds are being rebuilt in the harbor and seeded with oysters spawned in hatcheries. The Inner Harbor is now lined with restaurants and shops instead of canning factories and boats—but diners happily eat oysters on the half shell, with cocktail sauce on the side.

Baltimore Harbor is now a place of leisure rather than industry, playing host to cruise boats rather than a working fishing fleet.

# NEW YORK CITY

An aerial view of lower New York. Air force planes can be seen flying through the city skies.

Pollution was not on anyone's mind at the beginning of the 20th century, when the nation was reaping the benefits of a newly industrialized society. Despite obvious signs of trouble—harbors were full of oil waste and sewage and cities were shrouded in black smoke—very few people were concerned. As Commerce Secretary Herbert Hoover wrote in 1924: "Official Washington has no knowledge that the American people give a damn about pollution, and until they do care, there will be no great advance as to pollution."

The Public Health Service did begin surveying air pollution in eastern U.S. cities in 1928, reporting that sunlight was cut by 20 to 50 percent in New York City. However, reform did not gather momentum until later—in 1939, the smog was so thick in St Louis that lanterns were needed during daylight for a week, and in 1953 New York smog killed over 170 people. In 1963, Congress passed the Clean Air Act, with $95 million allocated for study and cleanup efforts.

Since then, the air in New York City and around the country has become cleaner and safer, and microscopic soot particles have declined by 30 percent since 1980. However, 121 million Americans still live in urban areas where the air is unhealthy. The World Trade Center bombings in Manhattan on September 11, 2001, left many concerned that burning debris and methane gas would cause health problems, but repeated testing showed no toxic pollutants.

The smoking hole left in the Manhattan skyline by the collapse of the World Trade Center after the September 11 terrorist attacks.

Camp George Washington, inhabited by veterans of the Civil War, in the grounds of the Washington Monument.

# WASHINGTON 1887

Although no one in the 19th century disputed that George Washington was the father of the United States and deserved a memorial, fate continually thwarted the project. The Washington National Monument Society was created in 1833 and approved a design by architect Robert Mills, complete with an obelisk surrounded by an ornate Greco-Roman temple. Fundraising took years, the earth sank under the original site, and when the Civil War erupted work stopped altogether. Abandoned at 150 feet, the monument sat untouched until 1880.

When work resumed, G.P. Marsh suggested design changes that would make the obelisk more like a classic Egyptian one, with a height-to-base ratio of 10 to 1. The final design called for a monument 555 feet tall, and the temple was abandoned. The monument was completed in 1885, but did not open to the public until 1888, when a steam hoist elevator was installed.

A million visitors a year now come to the Washington Monument, the focal point of the capital city. People used to be allowed to walk up the 897 steps to the top, but park officials closed them in 1971, concerned over wear and tear. The original elevator has long since been replaced, and instead there is now an elevator with windows.

The Washington Monument reflected on the surface of the Vietnam Memorial.

# NEW ORLEANS

Jazz was born over 100 years ago in New Orleans. Military bands were returning to port at the end of the Spanish–American war, flooding the city with used band instruments. African-Americans quickly bought up hundreds of the instruments and began to form bands. Many musicians could not read music, so instead they used existing melodies as a departure point for spontaneous playing. Not bound by European traditions, these early jazz bands played loosely structured melodies with improvised harmony and rhythm. Louis Armstrong was discovered in New Orleans, as were Jelly Roll Morton and countless others.

New Orleans today is still famous for its musical tradition, and city streets are often the venue for impromptu ensembles as well as formal marching bands. Scores of festivals feature music prominently. The New Orleans Jazz and Heritage Festival is held every spring and hosts hundreds of musicians ranging from jazz to blues to pop.

A formal marching band playing in the street during a carnival pageant in New Orleans, Louisiana.

Musicians and spectators enjoy the atmosphere at one of New Orleans' many festivals.

Streetcars were first introduced in San Francisco to cope with the steepness of Nob Hill but quickly spread to other areas of the city.

One rainy spring day in San Francisco in 1869, Andrew Hallidie saw a terrible accident: a horse-drawn streetcar slid down a steep hill paved with wet cobblestones and five horses were dragged to their deaths. Hallidie, whose father had invented wire rope, knew there was a way to tame San Francisco's fearsome hills. Four years later, the city started the first cable car railway system near the top of Nob Hill, and over the next quarter century opened many other cable car lines to serve its citizens.

In 1906, however, San Francisco's Great Earthquake struck. With the streets torn asunder, officials took the opportunity to convert many of the streetcars from cable to electric. Buses replaced other cable cars. They disappeared one by one until 1947, when San Francisco's mayor tried to shut down the system completely.

Fortunately, a group of concerned residents stopped him. The Citizens Committee to Save the Cable Cars authored a charter that forced the city to maintain and operate the cable cars. In 1964 the system was designated a special "moving" National Historic Landmark. Not too long ago, the first woman operated a cable car after she developed the huge upper body strength necessary for the grip and brakes. Riding to the top of Nob Hill in a streetcar today is a delight—one you will find only in San Francisco.

San Francisco's streetcars have been designated a National Historic Landmark.

173

When oil was discovered and the Depression held the country in its grip, Venice's once-beautiful beachfront became scarred with oilfields.

Venice, California, was built to resemble its Italian namesake, complete with romantic canals crisscrossing the city. During the Depression, however, when oil was discovered, American practicality promptly replaced Italian romance. Citizens voted to rezone the area to allow drilling, and by 1931 there were 340 oil wells lining the canals.

The once fashionable residential area turned noisy, smelly, and ugly. The city closed a school in the area and transferred the children. However, as oil production began to decline and the wells were pumped dry, the oil derricks were slowly removed and people began to resettle. The last derrick was dismantled in 1962.

Venice's rebirth came in the late 1960s, when flower children made it their home. In 1972, the city built a bike path through to Santa Monica, which drew thousands of rollerbladers. Today, the wide, open beaches, palm trees, and boardwalk make Venice a popular tourist destination.

The last oil derrick in Venice was dismantled in 1962 and the area has now regained its original beauty, in keeping with its romantic Italian namesake.

A section of the coastline of Miami following the great hurricane that brought an end to the Florida land boom.

# FLORIDA 1926

The 1926 hurricane in Florida—storms were not routinely given names until the 1950s—was the most destructive in U.S. history up to that point. The death toll was estimated to be between 325 and 800. Most of the residents living in the storm's path were recent arrivals to Florida, lured by the land boom and having no experience of the fury of the winds and the seas. Many of the deaths were caused when people unwittingly went out into the eye of the storm, believing the hurricane was over.

Most remarkable was the fact that hardly anyone knew the storm was coming. Newspapers ran a storm advisory that morning, but few took notice. The Weather Bureau in Washington, D.C., issued a hurricane warning at 6 p.m., but Miami weathermen had few ways of spreading the word—there was only one radio station in southern Florida and almost no one had a radio.

The contrast today is stark. Despite increased hurricane activity during the 1990s due to warmer seas, forecasters are now much better able to predict storms and communicate the danger. New computer modeling systems and better information from weather balloons are important recent developments. Hurricane Andrew, a 1992 storm that is currently the costliest on record, is a case in point—although it caused $25 billion in property damage, only 56 lives were lost.

Every cloud has a silver lining—children skating along a road use garbage bags as sails during a tropical storm in West Palm Beach, Florida.

The Custom House, a Boston icon, is as impressive today as it was when it was first built. Constructed at the end of the city docks, it was designed for the inspection and registration of cargo coming in on boats. Originally a four-story Greek temple topped with a dome, it has 36 Doric granite columns, each made from a single 46-ton piece of Quincy granite.

Then, in 1915, the Custom House took on a new look when a skyscraper was erected on top of it. Boston zoning regulations at that time prohibited tall buildings, but the federal government was exempt, and so it tore off the roof and added a 30-story tower with a 22-foot wide clock. Remarkably, the original temple does not clash with the Italian Renaissance tower.

The building's most recent incarnation is as a time-share condominium unit owned by Marriott Vacation Club International. Marriott bought the tower in 1995, and converted it while managing to retain the building's historic value. In addition to refurbishing the clock, observation deck, and rotunda, the new owners also preserved the habitat of two peregrine falcons living in the structure.

The Boston Custom House at the end of Commercial Street was once the only skyscraper in the area.

Although the restrictions on tall buildings in the area have now been relaxed, the tower of the Custom House still dominates downtown Boston.

Seattle's Space Needle and monorail were both built for the 1962 World's Fair, for which the theme was Century 21. Unlike many other structures built for world fairs, however, both are still in full use today and are defining elements of the city's skyline.

The Space Needle was originally topped by a balloon shape, but the final design sported the now-famous flying saucer. The five-level top dome houses a revolving restaurant and an observation deck that, some 50 years after the World's Fair, is still Seattle's top tourist destination.

The monorail was thought to represent the future of mass transit when it opened in 1962, the same year as the debut of the television show *The Jetsons*. Ironically, it is now the only publicly owned transit system in the United States that makes a profit. It covers the 0.9 mile distance between downtown Seattle and the World's Fair site in about two minutes, with a bullet-like passage through a music museum inspired by Seattle-born Jimi Hendrix. Seattle voters have been clamoring in recent years to extend the monorail into a full-fledged 40-mile system, with 22 stations spread across the city.

Aerial views of Seattle prior to the World's Fair (right) and today (far right), showing the Space Needle, and the monorail snaking through the downtown.

A construction worker balances on the end of a joist during the erection of the Lincoln-Liberty building (now the PNB-First Union building), where the Founder's Bell is located. The clock tower of Philadelphia City Hall is in the background.

The Founder's Bell rings the hours daily from its perch in a belfry atop the PNB-First Union building in Philadelphia, even though many mistakenly believe the sound comes from nearby City Hall. The bell was originally commissioned by Rodman Wanamaker in 1926 as a memorial to his father, a department store magnate, and also as a tribute to the 150 years of independence of the United States. The bell sounds a low "D" and weighs 15 tons—one ton for each decade since the Declaration of Independence was adopted.

Philadelphia holds a particularly special place in American history. In addition to being the country's first capital from 1790 to 1800, and the country's largest city between 1800 and 1830, it also had the nation's first public school, the first volunteer fire department, the first bank, the first stock exchange, and the first abolition of slavery act. In fact, Philadelphia's most famous bell, the Liberty Bell, became a national icon in 1837 when abolitionists adopted the cracked bell as a symbol for their movement. Today, the Liberty Bell is "rung" every Fourth of July to celebrate the nation's beginnings.

The statue of William Penn, founder of Pennsylvania, on top of City Hall is a focal point of downtown Philadelphia.

everyday living

# VACCINATION

Franklin D. Roosevelt was perhaps the world's most famous polio victim. Up until the 1960s there were several thousand cases of polio every year.

Polio is caused by three strains of virus, and can ultimately cause paralysis of the limbs or lungs. There was an outbreak of this highly contagious disease in the first half of the 20th century because, as sanitation improved, infants were no longer exposed to the virus at an early age, when the antibodies passed to them through their mother's milk gave them protection. Exposed to the polio virus later in life, they were at greater risk of contracting it.

In response to the outbreak, the March of Dimes Birth Defects Foundation enlisted Dr. Jonas Salk to develop a vaccine. Massive testing of the vaccine in clinical trails began in 1954. The following year, the dramatic results of the trials prompted the United States government to grant permission for the vaccine to be given to all children. By 1965, only 61 cases of paralytic polio were reported in the U.S. In 1994, polio was declared eradicated from all of the Americas. Vaccinations for a variety of childhood diseases are now routinely administered in schools throughout the country.

Film star Judy Holliday, who was a polio victim as a youngster, showing a vial of the new trial polio vaccine to the four-year-old poster boy for the March of Dimes Birth Defects Foundation.

HELP NOW!

RESEARCH WILL WIN

MARCH OF DIMES

An elementary school student in Kentucky receiving a vaccine.

The story of Wilbur and Orville Wright epitomizes American pluck and ingenuity. Inspired by a childhood fascination with flight, the brothers invented each of the technologies necessary to pursue their dream. Five of the seven early flying machines they built were failures, yet they persevered and learned from their mistakes.

In 1903 they developed the Flyer, a skeleton built of spruce, ash, and muslin that weighed just over 600 pounds. On December 17, Kitty Hawk, North Carolina, with Orville at the controls, the Flyer stayed aloft for 12 seconds. The next day only four newspapers carried the story—and most people thought the news was exaggerated.

With the invention of the airplane, Wilbur and Orville Wright created one of the greatest cultural forces of our time. Family members separated by oceans no longer needed to be strangers. Distant cultures are not so alien. War between countries halfway across the earth is possible. Globalization and an international economy are realities. The Wright brothers did more than invent the airplane—they changed our world.

Wilbur Wright watches his brother Orville fly the airplane they invented together at Kitty Hawk, North Carolina.

A jet landing at sunset in Los Angeles. Modern airplanes have come a long way since the Wright brothers' maiden 12-second flight at the beginning of the 20th century.

The idea of train travel still conjures visions of Pullman cars, fine dining, and the excitement of being whisked somewhere far away, even though fewer and fewer people today are making train trips.

The steam engine "Tom Thumb" pulled its first passenger car 13 miles from Baltimore to Ellicott's Mill, Maryland, in 1830, and in 1869 the Transcontinental Railroad was completed. During the golden age of railroads, between 1865 and 1916, trains offered the fastest, safest means of travel for Americans. Railroads moved cattle and freight as well as people, and were integral in the development of the United States.

During the 1940s, passenger trains began a losing battle with cars and airplanes, and even the creation of federally subsidized Amtrak in 1970 has failed to reverse the trend. It is hoped that the new, high-speed Acela trains, which began running in the Northeast Corridor in 2001, will bring back the elegance of passenger train travel. The new trains will substantially reduce travel time between cities, but just as important are amenities such as laptop plug-ins at each seat, and baby-changing tables in the bathrooms.

The evocative sight of steam trains lighting up the tracks at a Chicago station.

An Acela train at Boston's South Station. The new trains contain amenities such as laptop plug-ins and baby-changing tables.

## 1920

# MAN AND MACHINE

At the turn of the century, the American economy was dominated by industry and manufacturing. The work was often dangerous and conditions were terrible, yet the workers were usually unskilled laborers with little power to make change. Photographer Lewis W. Hine used his camera to document these atrocities and then brought his pictures to social welfare agencies to persuade them of the need for reform. The results of his efforts eventually led to the passage of safety and child labor laws.

Hine continued taking photographs of workers, however, and by the 1920s he became convinced that emerging technologies would reduce the amount of hard labor necessary to perform a job. He stopped seeing workers as victims, and he began a series of photographs that he called "Work Portraits," which showed man and machine in harmony, at work together.

Today, as machines continue to raise manufacturing productivity, mechanics who can service these machines are invaluable. Hine was prescient, however, for now manufacturing accounts for only 19 percent of the total jobs in the United States, versus the service industry, which accounts for 81 percent of employment.

Man and Steel by Lewis Hine (right). A power house mechanic working on steam pump (far right).

A firefighter operates a hose from the top of his engine. Technological advances in firefighting equipment have taken place throughout the past century to help firefighters do their work as effectively and safely as possible.

# FIREFIGHTERS

On September 11, 2001, terrorists flew planes into the twin towers of the World Trade Center in New York City, causing the towers to collapse and 2,843 people to die. However, the remarkable thing is not how many people died that day, but the number of people who survived. Some estimate that over 20,000 people were evacuated to safety, thanks in large part to the city's firefighters. Of the dead, 343 were firefighters killed in the line of duty.

The actions of firefighters on September 11 were heroic. That day highlighted the fact that every day, firefighters scattered all over the country, in situations terrifying and mundane, perform heroically. Over the last century, the development of better equipment has improved both the chances of beating the fire and safety for the firefighters. Bravery comes from the heart, however, and that has not changed at all.

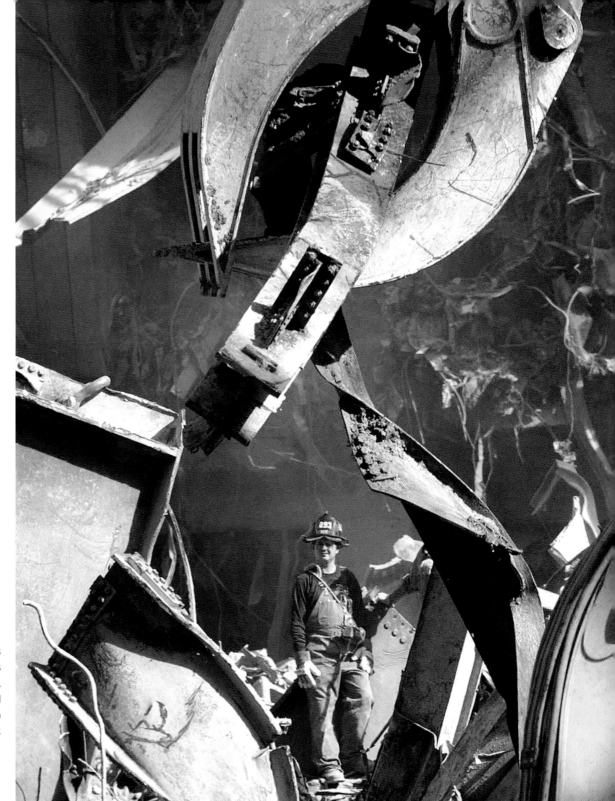

A firefighter looks on as heavy machinery removes debris from Ground Zero, the site of the collapsed World Trade Center in New York City.

## 1930

## MAIL CARRIERS

Believe it or not, the mail was not always delivered. City dwellers began getting mail delivery at their homes during the Civil War, when an Ohio postal clerk could no longer bear watching families receive tragic news about loved ones in the public hall of the post office. However, for decades after, some 30 million rural Americans had to travel miles to post offices to collect their mail.

Rural Free Delivery began in 1896, despite the fact that Congress had stalled for years, fearing that it would cost too much to build new, solid roads and hire more postal employees. Mail delivery changed farmers' lives, giving them regular access to newspapers and magazines from distant cities, and broadening their view of the world. Mail-order catalogs such as Montgomery Ward and Sears Roebuck allowed farmers to buy items that the local general store did not have.

Letter carriers today remain an integral part of the community. Many people know their letter carrier, and some stop to chat. They also fully understand the duties of their carrier, unlike one customer in the early days of rural mail delivery who left the following note on her stoop: "Please feed our chickens and water the cows and the mule in the stable. And if the bees have swarmed, put them in a new hive. We have gone visiting.

A letter carrier delivering mail on a rural route in Maine (far left) and a town delivery in Virginia (left).

197

# MILK DELIVERY

Today, having milk delivered to your door is for the finicky or the privileged. Most of us simply grab a plastic gallon off the convenience store shelf. However, not so long ago, milk came in round glass bottles from the back of a horse-drawn wagon that stopped at your home every morning before dawn.

The horse knew each house on the route and did not have to be told where to stop, and would wait until the milkman climbed back on board before going a little farther down the street. Every house had an insulated box on the porch to keep the milk cold in summer and to prevent it from freezing in winter. Rich, heavy cream would rise in the necks of the bottles, which customers would pour off and perhaps use for coffee.

Now, milk comes from milk factories, which buy unprocessed milk and cream from local farmers and use sophisticated transportation systems to deliver it to distant markets. It is homogenized, to break the fat globules up into minute particles, and pasteurized, to kill any harmful bacteria.

There is no doubt that modernization has improved the safety of milk and increased the choices for consumers—but if only that milk could be delivered by horse-drawn wagons in cold, glass bottles ...

A milkman proudly poses next to his horse-drawn wagon in Champaign, Illinois.

A father and daughter select a gallon of milk while shopping in a Walnut Creek grocery store in California.

ASSEMBLY LINE

Workers trying out the new Ford motor car assembly line in Detroit, Michigan.

A factory worker at the Ford assembly plant in Chicago, Illinois.

Up until 1908, automobiles were expensive, custom-made machines. Henry Ford wanted to create "a motor car for the great multitude," and so he designed the Model T, a simple, sturdy car that offered no choices at all—not even color. At a price of $850, the Model T was much less expensive than other cars, which cost around $2,000. The car was so popular that Ford was unable to keep up with the demand.

Ford realized he needed a more efficient way to produce the car. Inspired by a grain conveyer belt, he got the idea of moving parts to people instead of vice versa. He divided the assembly of the Model T into 84 distinct steps, so that workers could focus on performing one task well. Improved machinery and cutting tools produced standardized parts that could be used interchangeably. He also coached workers about the best way to perform their tasks, to reduce wasted time and effort.

All of this came together in 1913 with the first moving assembly line. The time it took to build the chassis went from 12½ to 1½ hours. The new system produced cars so efficiently that it cost less to build them. In 1915, Ford dropped the price of the Model T to $290, and sales jumped to 1 million cars. As well as revolutionizing the way we make cars and how much they cost, Ford's manufacturing principles were adopted by countless other industries, changing the working practices of the nation.

Sitting in regimented rows with hands folded neatly on the desktop to keep them from fiddling, these school children listen obediently to the teacher in this Maine classroom.

## SCHOOL 1959

Walk into an elementary school classroom and take a look at the desk arrangement—it will tell a lot about the teacher and how he or she runs the class. Back in the 1950s, however, everyone had classrooms set up the same way. The children's desks were in straight rows facing the front, where the teacher had a big desk. This was suited to the teaching style of the time: teachers talked, students listened; teachers wrote on the blackboard, students copied it on paper. Hands were folded primly on desktops to keep them from being too busy.

Classrooms are now less structured than in the past, reflecting a more informal student–teacher relationship. Teaching has also evolved so that instruction is more interactive, relying less on memorization and more on involving the student in hands-on learning. The battle axes of the past have given way to the battle cry of today: "learning is fun."

Modern teaching methods favor a more informal, interactive approach than in the past. This teacher in a school in Rensselaer, New York, encourages the children to participate as she teaches them to read.

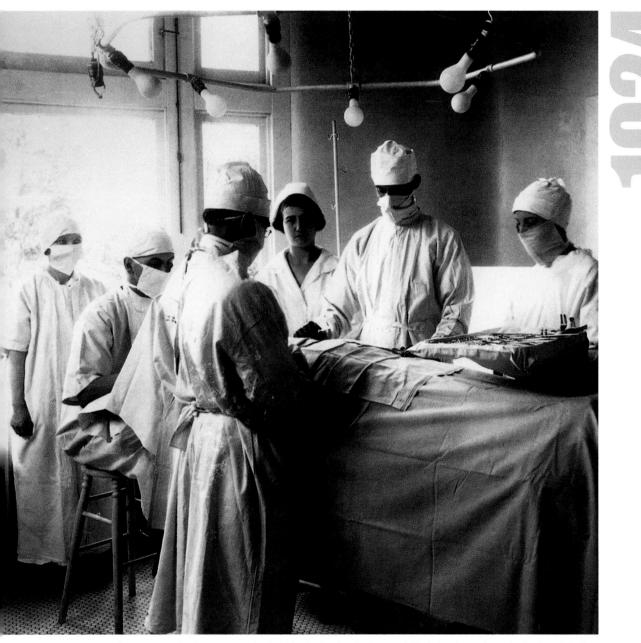
Surgeons conducting an operation in Idaho in the days before penicillin helped to reduce deaths from infection.

Medical care has improved remarkably in the last hundred years. Major revolutions in medicine—from antibiotics to X-rays—have increased our average life span from 47 years at the beginning of the 20th century to 77 years today.

The operating room in particular has become a safer place. Before the discovery of antibiotics, infection was one of the biggest causes of death. In the 1920s, President Calvin Coolidge watched helplessly as his 16-year-old son died of septic poisoning from a blister on his toe. Penicillin was discovered in 1928, but it was not widely used until World War II, when surgeons realized it lowered the chance of bacteria contaminating the wounds.

The discovery of X-rays has led to better imaging techniques, including the three-dimensional CT scan. Magnetic resonance imaging (MRI) followed soon after, giving a better view of the brain, spinal cord, and soft tissues. Combining these images with more sophisticated computers will soon allow surgeons to create a "virtual you" so that they can rehearse your operation before making a single cut—now that's progress.

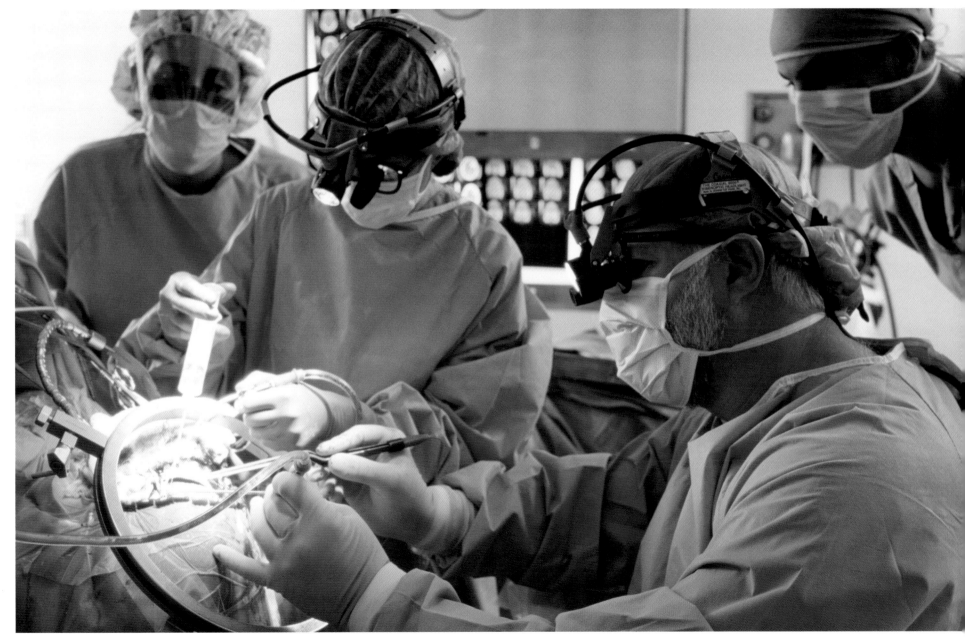

Doctors at the Chicago Institute of Neurosurgery and Neuroresearch operate on a brain using a "viewing wand" that transmits pictures to a television monitor.

## GETTING A TICKET

One has to wonder what the speed limit could have been if a police officer on a bicycle was able to catch up with this vehicle and give the driver a ticket.

America's car culture spawned another facet of everyday life: getting a ticket. Back in 1909, the state of Washington introduced the first speed limit of 12 miles per hour. In the early days, states set their own speed limits, although Montana and Nevada had no upper limit at all. Our elders got that same sinking feeling that we do today when the police officer waves down our car.

Now there is a backlash against writing tickets, with most people agreeing that tickets do not improve road safety. From 1966 to 1998 fatality rates on the road dropped steadily—despite the fact that police departments preoccupied with other more serious crimes were writing fewer tickets than ever. Some police chiefs are advocating that officers shift their focus to use traffic enforcement primarily as a means to discover more serious offenses.

If you do get stopped, there are a few things you can do to beat the rap. Ask for a warning instead of a ticket, and don't be afraid to say you are sorry. If the officer does not relent, show up in court and plead not guilty—chances are your fine will be reduced.

A highway patrol officer issues a ticket to a motorcyclist on the side of a road in Monterey, California.

# 1908

## TELEPHONE OPERATORS 1908

When telephones were first invented, companies hired teenage boys to be operators because of their success in working in telegraph offices. However, the boys tended to be rambunctious and pulled pranks on callers. In 1878 the Boston Telephone Despatch Company began hiring women operators, and by 1900 almost all operators were women.

Up until that time, the only jobs open to women were servant, factory worker, sales clerk, nurse, or teacher, so despite the low wages (about $7 a week), women flocked to the hiring office. To qualify, an operator had to be unmarried, aged 17 to 26, and have arms long enough to reach the phone lines. Her job was to plug a caller's phone line into the line of the person being called.

Over the next five decades, having a telephone went from being a rich person's luxury to every family's necessity. Long-distance service was established and transmission quality improved. Automatic switching systems reduced the need for operators. In 1983, the first cellular phones were available for sale in America, and now over 80 million cell phone users exist nationwide. Ironically, if you do need to dial information, chances are pretty good that the operator will be a man.

The telephone exchange in Hamburg, New York.

A modern businesswoman using a cellular telephone.

## STEAMBOATS 1909

Steamboats have long since been replaced by other methods of transportation, yet they hold an important place in the heart and history of the United States. Mark Twain's classic book *Life on the Mississippi* portrayed steamboats as the home of gamblers, dashing captains, and sly confidence men. More importantly, they played a critical role in helping pioneers settle land around the Mississippi River in the mid-1800s. In their heyday, some 9,000 steamboats plied the great river, serving as packets, showboats, ferries, towboats, and gunboats.

Adding to the romance was the fact that steamboats were dangerous. Some 4,000 people were killed during the four decades after they were introduced. Many captains, knowing that there were bets to be won, raced their boats. Safety was forsaken, as speeding boats crashed into underwater obstacles or even one another as the channel narrowed. Overheated boilers sometimes exploded, turning the wooden boats into raging bonfires. In fact, a boiler explosion killed Henry Clemens, Mark Twain's brother, in 1858.

Other forms of transportation such as the railroad replaced steamboats, and today only a handful still exist—all used as cruise boats for tourists. These giant, floating wedding cakes are festive with chandeliers, dance music, and river lovers—not unlike times past.

Mississippi River steamboats jostle for landing space in St. Louis, Missouri.

The *Belle Angela* is one of the few steamboats left on the Mississippi River. Festooned with lights and looking like a giant floating wedding cake, it conjures up images of a more romantic era.

OIL 1898

An oil derrick in California's Kern County. The area would soon be littered with thousands of wooden oil derricks like this one.

The oil industry has come a long way since the Pennsylvania Rock Oil Company first successfully drilled for oil in 1859. By the start of the 20th century, early entrepreneurs seeking black gold were creating boom towns in Texas, Oklahoma, Louisiana, and California. At one point in the mid-1920s, for example, over 7,000 wooden derricks covered the landscape in Kern County, California.

In the almost 150 years since the first U.S. oil well was drilled, however, many have gone dry. That, combined with fluctuating oil prices, has created a boom-and-bust cycle for oil-dependent cities and their populations. Experts say that we are not running out of oil—we are just running out of oil that is easy to extract from the ground.

Petroleum scientists are working on new ways to coax the remaining oil from underground reservoirs. Companies have begun experimenting with chemicals that act like soap to wash out the remaining oil, and with tiny living organisms that can free oil from reservoir rock. The success of these new methods will determine how much oil costs in the years ahead, and how much longer United States oil can meet the growing needs of the population.

A puller crew for an oil well service company pulls tubing from a new oil well near Hobbs, New Mexico.

213

A self-sufficient existence working on the land has always represented an ideal way of life for many Americans, but farming also entails many hardships.

Free land and an abundance of natural resources had a profound impact on shaping the democratic society of America. Vast amounts of farmland drew many immigrants to the United States in the 19th century, and spurred continued westward migration. Early pioneer settlers were self-sufficient farmers, who built their own buildings, sewed clothing, raised livestock, and grew their own food—all with few mechanical tools. Despite the hardships, farming represented an ideal way of life built on ingenuity and equality.

Farming still represents an American ideal, but the globalization of world food production has meant that the nation's small farmers are having a hard time making a living. Large systems of crop subsidies abroad make it cheaper to import certain items into the country rather than grow them. Meanwhile, in an effort to provide a safety net for U.S. farmers, the government has its own system of subsidies that can encourage overproduction. This leads to lower prices, which hurt smaller farmers the most.

Large industrialized farms can now be found throughout the United States and are a far cry from the small homesteads of the early pioneers.

A woman working in the U.S. Department of Agriculture's laboratory of plant pathology in Washington, D.C.

# 1916

## WOMEN IN SCIENCE

A Nobel Prize was first awarded to a woman in 1903, only two years after the Nobel Foundation was first established—Marie Curie won it for Physics. Women have been winning Nobel Prizes ever since, and have done so in all categories except Economics.

However, the fact remains that women are disproportionately underrepresented in science. According to a recent report by the National Science Foundation, women scientists and engineers receive a minority of doctorates in all fields except psychology, are less likely than men to hold high-ranking positions in colleges and universities, and are less well paid than men.

Fortunately, younger women are now joining the ranks of career scientists at a growing rate. For example, women as a percentage of people receiving doctoral degrees increased from 26 percent in 1985 to 31 percent in 1995. In addition, the salaries of men and women within younger age categories are now close to comparable.

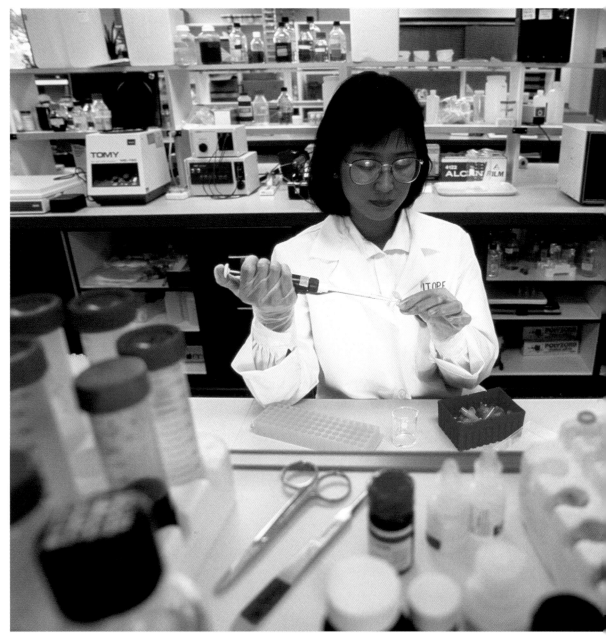

A female researcher at her workbench in a biochemistry laboratory.

Businessmen sit around a boardroom table and listen in as the president of telecommunications giant AT&T officially opens radio-telephone service to London, England

Although the fundamentals behind corporate business meetings have not changed, their trappings have altered substantially in the last decades. Gone are the suits and ties, replaced by khakis and sweaters. Gone is the deferential treatment of the boss, replaced by jovial camaraderie all around. Cell phones now interrupt the once focused proceedings.

Even business meetings are now being replaced, at times, by video conferencing. The recent threat of terrorism sparked an upsurge in video conferencing due to people's reluctance to fly. The technology has been available for years, but poor sound and picture quality deterred many. High-speed networks now allow much higher quality video links to be established.

However, video conferencing will never replace the need for face-to-face meetings. Just as in days gone by, there are times when a handshake and looking someone in the eye are needed to close the deal.

Technology continues to change the face of business. Meetings via video conference are no longer unusual.

Perched precariously high in the sky, this construction worker helps build the Empire State Building, which took the title of world's tallest building from the Chrysler skyscraper (visible on the right).

The Empire State Building was completed in 1930 in an astonishingly short period of time—just 1 year and 45 days. Construction workers were on the job all week, including Sundays and holidays. Workplace safety was unheard of, and men skipped about on exposed steel girders hundreds of feet above the ground. When placing a foot wrong meant certain death, it is remarkable that only two men fell and died during construction.

The Empire State Building stole the title of tallest building in the world from the Chrysler Building, and it remained the tallest building in the world for 40 years, until the World Trade Center was built in lower Manhattan. Today, the competition to build "the world's tallest" continues. The most ambitious proposal is for a 4,029 foot Bionic Tower in Hong Kong, which would be 300 storeys tall. Fortunately, new laws protect construction workers more than ever before—they need it.

Safety measures for construction workers are now enforced by law.

221

# WALL STREET

Wall Street originally got its start as a dirt path in front of Trinity Church in lower Manhattan over 200 years ago. Although the idea of stocks had not yet been invented, people were willing to pay silver for certificates giving them the right to profits from cargo coming in off boats in the harbor. Before long, banks were starting to sell shares to raise money, and the essence of the modern-day stock market was born. In 1792 the New York Stock Exchange (NYSE) set up shop in their first home, at 40 Wall Street.

Today, the New York Stock Exchange has been joined by the American Stock Exchange, NASDAQ, and hundreds of other local and international exchanges that all play a critical role in the worldwide economy. The 36,000 square foot trading floor at the NYSE is designed so that buy and sell orders for a specific stock all come to one person—ensuring that the price will be set by the interplay of supply and demand. These individuals, known as specialists, are supported by a host of technological tools, which means that about 2.5 billion shares can be traded on the floor per day.

People crowd Wall Street after the Stock Market Crash of 1929. An extra 400 police officers were dispatched to guard the area.

A host of technological tools ensures the efficient trading of 2.5 billion shares per day on Wall Street.

# celebrations

# GRADUATION

A graduating class from Radcliffe College in Cambridge, Massachusetts, gather together outside a college building to pose for a group photograph.

Some think that graduation is a solemn and important occasion, while others cannot wait to toss their cap in the air and run out screaming. Either way, graduation is a rite of passage, a ritual that marks the beginnings of adulthood and the responsibilities that come with that new status.

The familiar trappings include class rings, diplomas, caps, and gowns. The first class ring was developed by West Point students in 1837. The engraving on the ring showed a book with a sword driven through it to symbolize the students' contempt for their textbook on artillery. Today, rings are worn to demonstrate school spirit and as a public display of having earned a diploma.

The custom of wearing a cap and gown dates back to the formation of early universities in Europe, when scholars wore long gowns to keep warm in unheated buildings. Today, the dress code is very strict: bachelor's degree gowns have pointed sleeves and are worn closed; master's degree gowns have oblong sleeves that open at the wrist; and doctorate degree gowns have bell-shaped sleeves. No matter what clothes the graduate has on, however, he or she is usually also wearing a smile.

Graduating students celebrate at New York City's Columbia University, one of the oldest institutes of higher education in the U.S.

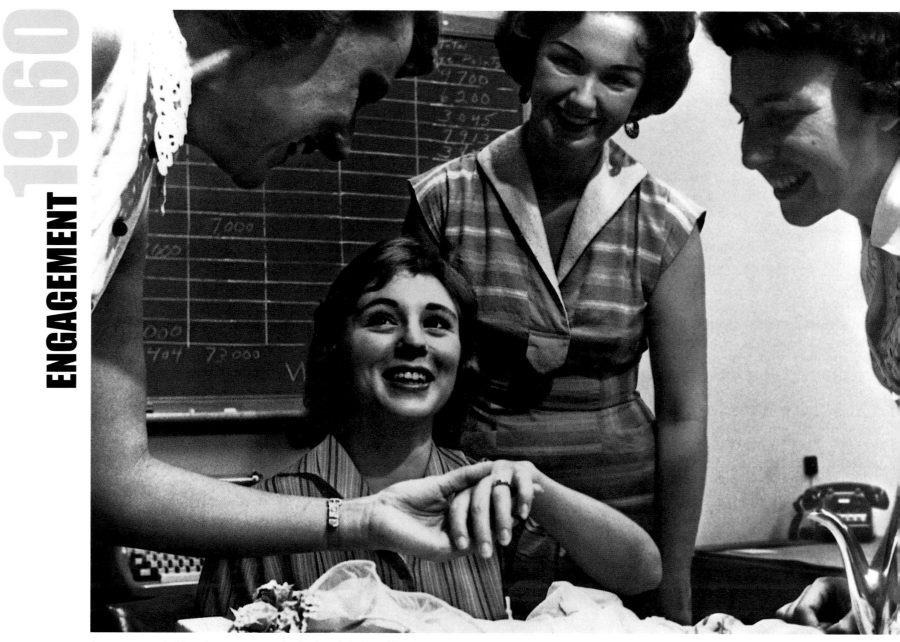

A young woman holds up her engagement ring for the admiration of friends at her bridal shower.

Deciding to become engaged is among the most important moments of a couple's lives together, but after family and friends have been told the good news, all too soon come the words, "Let me see the ring!"

The first diamond engagement ring was given to Mary of Burgundy in 1477 by Archduke Maximillian of Austria, but it was not until diamonds were discovered in Africa in 1870 that a wider public could afford to buy them. Wearing the ring on the fourth finger of the left hand dates back to ancient Egypt, when it was believed that the "vena amoris" ("the vein of love") ran from that finger directly to the heart.

Today, sporting an engagement ring is still seen as an important symbol of a couple's commitment to each other. Hands that have never seen fingernail polish before are held out, meticulously manicured, to display the prize. Some things have changed, however. Decades ago, women who were newly engaged were expected to drop out of the workforce so that they could focus on their marriage and the imminent arrival of children. Today, marriage does not signal an immediate lifestyle change, but the size of the rock in the ring is still important. "If it's under a carat, don't wear it," the saying goes, even though the average diamond engagement ring is actually half a carat.

Today, the engagement ring—or at least the size of the rock in the ring—is still the focus of attention whenever a woman gets engaged.

A wedding party in front of The Little Church Around the Corner in Manhattan.

## MARRIAGE 1966

Marriage is probably the most maligned institution on the face of the earth, yet people persevere. About 9 out of 10 people will marry at some point in their lifetime, which translates into 6,500 marriages per day in the United States. In fact, people are clamouring to be allowed to do it—gays and lesbians won an important battle in 1999 in the Vermont Supreme Court, which proclaimed that gay couples are entitled to the same legal benefits as straight married couples. Now, homosexuals are working toward legislation that will allow them to become legally married.

However, despite the popularity of marriage, data show that 43 percent of first marriages end in separation or divorce within 15 years. The most important factor leading to divorce is the age of the woman—the older she is, the longer the marriage is likely to last. Fortunately, women have been waiting longer to get married. The average age now is 25, versus 22 in 1980, and the divorce rate has been dropping steadily since 1993.

A gay couple on their wedding day in Manhattan. Although gay weddings are commonplace, to date they are not legally recognized.

A sailor blows his horn at V-J Day celebration in Times Square, New York City.

# VICTORY CELEBRATIONS

On September 2, 1945, America officially celebrated the end of World War II with V-J Day, "Victory over Japan." That day was a solemn one—over 292,000 Americans had lost their lives in the war, and over 1.3 million Japanese had died.

Three weeks earlier, the celebrations across the U.S. had been boisterous. In early August, the U.S. had dropped the atomic bomb on Hiroshima and Nagasaki, and on August 14, Japan's army agreed to surrender. That night, more than 2 million people poured into Times Square in New York City to celebrate. Across the country, people in cities and small towns alike turned out to kiss, dance, parade, and make noise.

Although the Persian Gulf War did not directly affect as many Americans as World War II, sentiments also ran strong. After a devastating air assault of targets held by Iraqi president Saddam Hussein in Iraq and Kuwait, ground troops defeated Saddam's soldiers in only four days. Cheering crowds greeted victory parades everywhere, and the New York City parade was the largest held since the end of World War II.

The Desert Storm victory parade in New York City celebrated the successful ground attack that ended the Persian Gulf War.

# INAUGURATION

The unfinished Capitol building in Washington, D.C., formed the backdrop to President Abraham Lincoln's inauguration.

Since the very first presidential inauguration—George Washington's in 1789—the ceremony has been deeply rooted in tradition. After saying the oath of office, Washington added the phrase "so help me God," and almost every president has said it since. Washington also started the tradition of giving an inaugural address after the swearing in. His address was the shortest in history at 135 words. The longest was by William Henry Harrison in 1841. It took one and half hours to deliver the 8,600-word address—in a driving ice storm. He died from pneumonia within a month.

In 1801 Thomas Jefferson was the first president to be inaugurated at the Capitol in Washington, D.C., which became the capital city that year. In 1861, President-elect Abraham Lincoln traveled in an open carriage with defeated president James Buchanan to the Capitol. The crowd gathered before the east portico of the still-unfinished Capitol to watch the swearing in. At Lincoln's inauguration in 1865, African-Americans marched in the inaugural parade for the first time.

The ceremony was held at the Capitol's East Front until 1981, when Ronald Reagan moved it to the West Front to reflect his connection with California. Subsequent presidents were inaugurated at the West Front as well, because there is more room for spectators. George W. Bush was sworn in as the 43rd president of the United States on January 20, 2001.

The inauguration of George W. Bush outside the West Front of the Capitol.

Santa Claus treats young visitors to a sleigh ride at his North Pole workshop in the Adirondack Mountains of New York.

Santa Claus began his life in America in the 1800s, when early Dutch settlers told the story of Sinter Klaas, a saint legendary for his gift-giving and love of children. The name originally appeared in American newspapers as St A. Claus, but he quickly became known as Santa Claus after Clement Clarke Moore wrote the immensely popular *The Night Before Christmas* in 1823. Important details such as reindeer names and the method for getting back up the chimney (laying a finger aside the nose) were included.

Thomas Nast, who illustrated Christmas issues of *Harper's Magazine* from the 1860s to the 1880s, was responsible for Santa's rotund shape, his North Pole workshop, and the list of good and bad children. However, it was really Haddon Sundblom who created Santa as we think of him today, with his fur-trimmed red suit, leather boots, and belt. From 1931 to 1964, Sundblom drew Santa for Coca-Cola advertisements that appeared worldwide on the back covers of the *Post* and *National Geographic* magazines.

Christmas today is too often associated with commerce, and the proliferation of Santas on street corners and in malls can be offputting. However, if you watch a child's face when you mention Santa Claus, the wonder of Christmas will magically reappear.

Santa Claus waves from amid the crowd on Waikiki Beach, Hawaii.

**NEW YEAR 1900**

Garlands of colored lights—powered by the new invention of electricity—were hung in New York City to celebrate the arrival of the 20th century.

The dawn of a new century often brings out unbridled optimism. Over 100 years ago, the new rear prompted a newspaper editorial proclaiming the wonders of "sanitation, surgery, drainage, plumbing, and every product of science and accessory of luxury. It seems impossible to imagine an improvement on what we have."

In New York City, revelers rang in the year 1900 downtown at City Hall. Electricity, which was brand new at the time, powered colored lights suspended from wires, and the assembled crowd sang a rousing version of the "Star Spangled Banner."

Four years later, the party moved uptown to Times Square for a New Year's celebration sponsored by *The New York Times* to inaugurate their new headquarters building. The first ball-lowering took place in 1907, and it has continued ever since. Some 500,000 people come to see it, and it is estimated that another 500 million watch it on television worldwide. The party to ring in 2001 featured a new ball made of Waterford crystal. It replaced the old ball, which was encrusted with 12,000 rhinestones.

Crowds of revelers wait for the ball to drop in Times Square, New York City, to signal the beginning of a new year.

# BIRTHDAYS

Birthday parties began long ago in Europe, when it was thought that evil spirits were attracted to people on their birthdays. Family and friends would come to ward off the spirits with good wishes and gifts. At first, only kings were considered important enough to warrant a celebration, but gradually children were included as well.

Over the years, birthday parties for children have changed. Parties used to be held at a child's home, with games such as pin the tail on the donkey or hide and seek. Today, many stressed parents choose to pay for parties at places like Leapin' Lizards or McDonalds, where food and entertainment are provided. Regardless of the location, cake usually makes an appearance, although often in the guise of ice cream cake or cupcakes. Candles are lit and blown out, and sometimes silly hats are worn. Like most of our other social occasions, birthday parties have become more casual as the years have passed, but they have not become less meaningful.

A young girl makes a wish and blows out the candles on her birthday cake.

Wearing a party hat and eager to taste the cake, this small boy enjoys his first birthday.

FOURTH OF JULY PARADE, NOME, ALASKA, 1911
Co's "B" 16 16TH INF. U.S.A. PASSING REVIEWING STAND

A group of soldiers marches down a street in Nome, Alaska, as part of the Fourth of July parade.

242

There are few things as American as the Fourth of July. Fireworks, parades, and barbecues have all been around for longer than the holiday itself, which was first celebrated after the Declaration of Independence was adopted by Congress on July 4, 1776. Williamsburg, Virginia, had a celebration on July 25, and Trenton, New Jersey, celebrated on July 26. Philadelphia hosted one of the most elaborate celebrations on July 4, 1777, replete with all the trappings of our modern-day events, including cannon firing, music, toasts, a parade, and fireworks.

Independence Day is one of only four American holidays celebrated on its actual calendar date—the others are Halloween, Christmas, and New Year. People have long insisted on celebrating the actual day, even when it falls on a Sunday. The July 18, 1777, edition of the *Virginia Gazette* stated the sentiment eloquently: "Thus may the Fourth of July, that glorious and ever memorable day, be celebrated through America, by the sons of freedom, from age to age till time shall be no more. Amen and Amen."

Children waving flags at a Fourth of July parade in Bristol, Vermont, to celebrate America's independence.

## HALLOWEEN 1917

Celebrated for centuries by ancient Celts and other Europeans with nature-based religions, Halloween is considered by most children to be the best night of the year. However, it was not always the fun, community-based holiday that it is today.

Early people believed that on October 31 the dead came back to Earth, and many of today's customs originate from the strategies our forebears designed to deal with ghosts. To avoid being recognized by the dead, people would wear masks when they left home after dark so that the ghosts would mistake them for their fellow spirits. To keep the ghosts from entering their homes, they placed bowls of food outside. Carved gourds or turnips lighted with glowing embers of coal were meant to frighten the spirits away.

Halloween was brought to America in the 1840s by waves of European immigrants, but it took nearly 100 years for it to evolve as we know it today. Community leaders urged parents to make the holiday less frightening, and by the turn of the century Halloween was celebrated with parties and parades. Now Americans spend almost $7 billion a year on Halloween candy, and fear comes not from ghosts, but from the amount of sugar consumed on a single evening.

Young boys carving faces into pumpkins to frighten away spirits on Halloween.

A boy tries to jump up and touch the mouth of a large illuminated pumpkin in Ellisville, Mississippi.

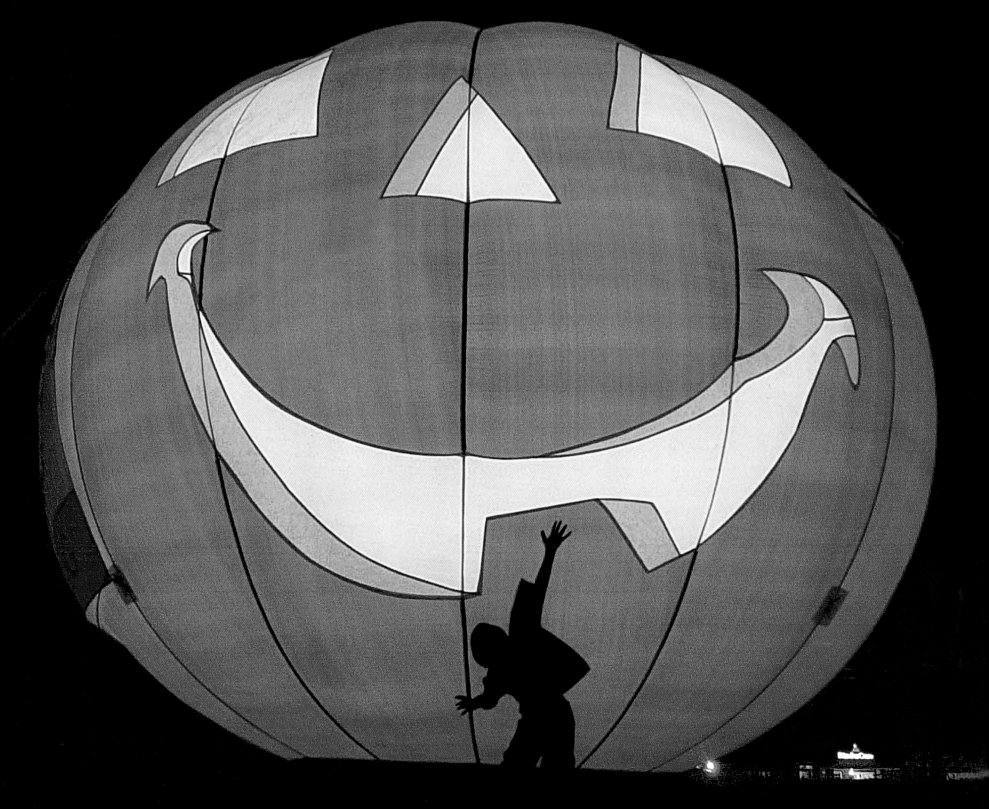

Elegantly dressed New
Yorkers parading along Fifth
Avenue on Easter morning.

## EASTER PARADE 1906

The Easter Parade grew from a custom started hundreds of years ago in the early days of the church, when those who were baptized on Holy Saturday were given new white robes to wear. Other congregation members wore new clothes to show their participation in Christ's rebirth, and after church everyone would march in a processional down the streets.

In 1860, Atlantic City, New Jersey, was the first American city to organize an Easter Parade, and New York's Fifth Avenue Easter Parade soon followed. Back then, the parade was a chance for people to show off their finery and their bonnets, and enjoy the spring sunshine after a long winter. Fifth Avenue, with its mansions and wide sidewalks, was the perfect parade ground.

These days the Fifth Avenue Easter Parade has a somewhat less refined air. So-called Easter bonnets are taken to an extreme that only New Yorkers can reach. Beyond the usual flowers, bonnets can sport live rabbits, pet snakes, clowns, and reproductions of famous artworks, like Leonardo da Vinci's *The Last Supper*.

Nowadays, the hats worn during the Easter Parade can be outlandish. Those pictured here, festooned with flowers and butterflies, are relatively sedate for New York.

# THANKSGIVING

President Franklin D. Roosevelt carving the turkey at a Thanksgiving dinner at the Warm Springs Foundation for infantile paralysis sufferers in Georgia.

Sometime between September 21 and November 11 in 1621, the Pilgrims and the Wampanoag Indians shared a harvest feast that is now commonly referred to as the first Thanksgiving. Although there was no specific day of thanksgiving set aside for many subsequent years, fall celebrations did continue and embraced good harvests as well as other events, including war victories and the new constitution. By the 1800s, an increasing number of states were celebrating annually, each on its own day.

President Abraham Lincoln proclaimed Thanksgiving a national holiday in 1863, designating the official day as the last Thursday in November. All of the following presidents made similar proclamations until Franklin D. Roosevelt in 1939 designated it as the third Thursday of November, hoping that a longer Christmas shopping season would spur the economy. It was changed back to the fourth Thursday two years later. Regardless of the date it is celebrated, Thanksgiving is often celebrated with overindulgence, just as it probably was back in 1621.

A family prepares to say a prayer of thanks before enjoying their Thanksgiving meal at a farmhouse in Weld County, Colorado.

# MACY'S PARADE

Since 1924, Macy's Thanksgiving Day Parade in New York City has synthesized family tradition with corporate hutzpah to produce one of the country's most anticipated Thanksgiving events. The parade began when Macy's employees, many of whom were first-generation immigrants, wanted to celebrate the holiday with fanfare. They marched from 145th Street down to 34th Street, dressed in costumes and accompanied by 25 animals borrowed from the Central Park Zoo.

Giant helium balloons first appeared in 1927 with Felix the Cat. Back then, the balloons were released at the end of the parade, floating for days until someone captured them and returned them for a prize. Wind is usually not a friend to the balloons, though—strong winds forced Mighty Mouse to the pavement in the 1956 parade, and even Bart Simpson suffered a big rip in his backside during the 1993 parade because of heavy gusts. The only time the parade has been canceled, in 1970, was due to a fierce gale.

A more recent tradition is watching the balloons being blown up the night before the parade. Visitors can wander the streets on the Upper West Side and see the giant cartoon characters lying on their sides, tethered with ropes, looking like they are trying to get a good night's sleep before the big day.

Huge balloons of characters such as Mighty Mouse (right) and Bart Simpson (far right) are paraded along the streets as part of Macy's Thanksgiving extravaganza.

A group of children are dressed in their best clothes for the New Year celebrations in New York's Chinatown.

The Chinese New Year is the most important celebration in the Chinese community. The date varies from year to year, because it is based on a lunar calendar, but it usually falls between January 20 and February 19. People wear red clothes, decorated with poems on red paper, and give children "lucky money" in red envelopes—red symbolizes fire, which is believed to drive away bad luck. The New Year's Eve feast traditionally includes seafood and dumplings, for happiness and family.

As the home of two of the largest Chinese communities in America, San Francisco and New York City have long hosted large Chinese New Year celebrations. The Dragon Parade in San Francisco is the biggest parade in the country, featuring floats, bands, stilt walkers, Chinese acrobats, and lion dancing. The highlight is the dragon dance, when a paper dragon hundreds of feet long is held aloft by young men as they dance through the streets.

New York hosts a similar parade, but in 1997 Mayor Rudulph Giuliani banned firecrackers from the lion dances, a ritual where dance troupes perform in stores along the streets to chase away evil and ensure prosperity. Since dancers had to perform until the last firecracker was out, storeowners would set off long belts of red firecrackers to ensure a long performance and greater prosperity. Without firecrackers, lion dances are disappearing from Chinese New Year celebrations in America.

Young boys carrying flags and wearing traditional red costumes during a Chinese New Year parade in San Francisco's Chinatown.

# INDEX

# PICTURE CREDITS

**The publishers would like to thank the following sources for their kind permission to reproduce the pictures in this book:**

**Allsport** 83, 117, 82, 91
**Corbis** 66, 92,168,178, 226, 234, /Tony Arruza 4/5, 19, 177, 241, /Craig Aurness 101, 211, /Bain News Services 252, /Nathan Benn 111, /Bettmann 4/5, 14, 20, 36, 44, 46, 52, 68, 70, 74, 78, 86, 100, 110, 112, 130, 140, 146, 180, 186, 198, 208, 218, 222, 230, 248, 250, /James P Blair 243, /Gary Braasch 131, /Lee Brothers 32, /Richard Cummins 11, 39, /Ecoscene 121, /Sandy Felsenthal 161, 201, /Kevin Fleming 109, 179, /Mark E Gibson 37, /Lynn Goldsmith 13, /Richard Hamilton Smith 99, /Rose Hartman 23, /Robert Holmes 75, /E O Hoppe 182, /Hulton 38, /Richard Hutchings 43, /Wolfgang Kaehler 4/5, 129, /Ken Kaminesky 209, /Catherine Karnow 41, 231, /Mike King 71, /Bob Krist 183, 187, /Michael S Lewis 249, /Robert Llewellyn 219, /Robert Maass 203, /James Marshall 247, /Michael Maslan Historic Photographs 242, /Buddy Mays 159, /Joe McDonald 155, /Wally McNamee 154,169, 235, /Bruce Miller 17, /Gail Mooney 251, /Kevin R Morris 4/5, 53, /Genevieve Naylor 106, /Douglas Peebles 237, /Caroline Penn 145, /Chris Rainier 4/5, 207, /Roger Ressmeyer 205, /Bob Rowan 141, 199, /George Rinhart 194, /Duomo/William

Sallaz 113, /Phil Schermeister 253, /Joseph Sohm 189, /Paul A Souders 147, /Vince Streano 79, /Ted Streshinsky 21, /JM Wait 76, /Ron Watts 193, /Nik Wheeler15, /Adam Woolfit 127, /Tim Wright 197, /Michael S Yamashita 45, 143,
**Getty Images News** 35, 69 /Bill Greenblatt 97, 245, /Chris Hondros 27, 239, /Lee K Marriner 105, /Darren McCollester 191, /David McNew 153, /Spencer Platt 227, /Joe Raedle 4/5, 63, 95, 167, /Alexander Sibaja 93, /Mario Tama 87, 163, 195, /Mark Wilson 55
**Hulton Archive** 6, 10, 16, 48, 96, 104, 108, 116, 134, 136, 142, 144, 148, 150, 152, 162, 170, 174, 176, 232, 236,
Imagebank 8/9, 50/1, 80/1, 118/9, 156/7, 184/5, 224/5, /Jurgen Vogt 149, 151
**ImageState** 29, 31, 33, 59, 61, 107, 165, 173, 223, /Joe Sohm 7 m, 77, 233
**Kobal Collection** 56
**Library of Congress** 4/5, 12, 18, 22, 30, 34, 60, 62, 88, 98, 124, 138, 202, 238, 240, 244
**Mary Evans Picture Library** 172
**NARA** 4/5, 24, 26, 58, 64, 84, 94, 158, 160, 164, 166, 190, 200, 204, 206, 210, 212, 214, 220, 228, 246, /George W Ackerman 196, /Ansel Adams

4/5, 122, 126, 128, /Everet F Bumgardner 2, 28, /Clinedinst Studio 216, /Lewis Hine 192, /Jacobs 102, /Walter J Lubken 120, /Staff Sgt Albert R Simpson 54, /Westinghouse Electric Corporation 42, /Orville Wright and John T Daniels 188,
**Picture Desk**/Neil Setchfield 123, 175
**Redferns**/David Redfern 171
**Rex Features** 90, 125, 137, 221, /Brendan Bierne 115 /Neale Haynes 89
Stone 4/5, 49, 135, 181, 215, 229, /Rich Iwasaki 217, /Jeff Mermelstein 47,
**Telegraph Colour Library**/Sean Sullivan 103
Timepix/Rex Features 85, 139, /Kimberly Butler 25, /Don Cravens 72, /Arnold H Drapkin 67, /Alfred Eisenstaedt 132, /Robert W Kelley 40, /Steve Liss 133, /Greg Mathieson/MAI 65, /Art Rickerby 114, /Diana Walker 73
**Topham**/ImageWorks 213, /PA 57

Every effort has been made to acknowledge correctly and contact the source and/or copyright holder of each picture, and Carlton Books Limited apologises for any unintentional errors or omissions which will be corrected in future editions of this book.